Francisco Balbi di Correggio was born in Correggio, in the Italian province of Emilio, in 1505. Little is known about his life, but he fought in the Spanish corps during the great siege of Malta at the age of sixty as an arquebusier. Shortly afterwards he wrote this historical narrative, which is the only first-hand account of the siege in existence. He died in 1589.

Ernle Bradford was born in Norfolk, in 1922, and was educated at Uppingham School. He joined the Royal Navy as a volunteer at eighteen and served with distinction for the duration of the Second World War. He was a broadcaster for the BBC and a magazine editor. He was a writer from the age of sixteen, and published numerous books, including *The Great Siege: Malta 1565* (1961), *Ulysses Found* (1963), *Cleopatra* (1971; Classic Penguin, 2000), *Mediterranean: Portrait of a Sea* (1971; Classic Penguin, 2000), *Christopher Columbus* (1973), *The Sword and the Scimitar: The Saga of the Crusades* (1974), *Hannibal* (1982), *Julius Caesar: The Pursuit of Power* (1984) and *Siege: Malta 1940–1943*. He lived in Malta with his family until his death in 1986.

GRAND MASTER LA VALETTE

Francisco Balbi di Correggio

THE SIEGE OF MALTA

1565

Translated from the
Spanish edition of 1568
by Ernle Bradford

PENGUIN BOOKS

PENGUIN BOOKS

Published by the Penguin Group
Penguin Books Ltd, 80 Strand, London WC2R ORL, England
Penguin Putnam Inc., 375 Hudson Street, New York, New York 10014, USA
Penguin Books Australia Ltd, 250 Camberwell Road, Camberwell, Victoria 3124, Australia
Penguin Books Canada Ltd, 10 Alcorn Avenue, Toronto, Ontario, Canada M4V 3B2
Penguin Books India (P) Ltd, 11 Community Centre, Panchsheel Park, New Delhi – 110 017, India
Penguin Books (NZ) Ltd, Cnr Rosedale and Airborne Roads, Albany, Auckland, New Zealand
Penguin Books (South Africa) (Pty) Ltd, 24 Sturdee Avenue, Rosebank 2196, South Africa

Penguin Books Ltd, Registered Offices: 80 Strand, London WC2R ORL, England

www.penguin.com

First published in Great Britain by The Folio Society Limited 1965
Published in Penguin Books 2003

1

Copyright © The Folio Society Limited, 1965
Maps drawn by K. C. Jordan
All rights reserved

Printed in England by Clays Ltd, St Ives plc

CONTENTS

ILLUSTRATIONS

With the exception of the frontispiece, the illustrations are from engravings made after the originals of Mateo Perez d'Aleccio, and were first published by Lucini in 1631.

INTRODUCTION

FRANCISCO BALBI DI CORREGGIO was a man of sixty when he fought as an arquebusier in the Spanish corps during the great siege of Malta. Two years later, in 1567, the first edition of his history of the siege was published in Alcala de Henares. The second edition, which was published in Barcelona in 1568, is the one which I have used for this translation. As Balbi himself makes clear, this second edition had been improved and amended on the suggestion of various knights and others. We may take it, then, that this is as accurate an account as was possible at the time. Of Balbi himself we know little, except that he was born in Correggio in the Italian province of Emilia in 1505. Sir Harry Luke has investigated the chronicles of the town and found the following entry for 12 December 1589: 'It is believed that the death of Francisco Balbi di Correggio, a wandering poet who wrote in Italian and Spanish and who was ever persecuted by men and by fortune, occurred on this date away from his native land. He is mentioned favourably by the celebrated Tiraboschi and by the historian Colleoni.'

The only other eye-witness to record the siege was Antonfrancesco Cirni, a Corsican cleric, who came to Malta with the main relief force in September 1565. His account, which has a number of details that are not recorded by Balbi, was compiled by him from the survivors of the siege. Unlike Balbi, he was not involved in the fighting, and it is to the latter that we must look for one of the very rare first-hand accounts of what it was like to be in the garrison of a besieged fortress during the sixteenth century.

Another who published an account of these events was Pierre Gentil de Vendôme, who came to Malta after the siege was over. So too did the famous Abbé de Brantôme, a man who was so much an admirer of the knights that, although not a member of the Order, he even embarked on several of their 'caravans' – expeditions in their armed galleys into the waters of the Levant and off the North African coast, to raid Turkish shipping. These, and other chroniclers, have added many details and individual incidents and stories, of which Balbi was unaware. They have also filled in a great deal of the political background which Balbi either did not know, or did not consider it wise to mention. For the battle for Malta was, like all

battles, determined primarily by political considerations. It was, indeed, one of the outstanding incidents in the Wars of Religion – and
it was this fact which lent so much bitterness to the struggle. But it
was also largely a matter of purely material considerations.

The Ottoman Empire which has been described as 'that military
state *par excellence* . . . built upon an ever-extending conquest', was
engaged in a deadly struggle with its Christian enemies. Forty-three
years before his attack on Malta, the Sultan Suleiman, then in the
prime of his youth, had driven the knights of the Order of St John
from their fortress home in the island of Rhodes. It had been in-
tolerable that these Christians should be allowed to remain in the
waters of the Aegean Sea, leaning like a spear against the side of the
Turkish coast.

Balbi, in his introduction to the story of the siege, tells the history
of the knights during these wandering years. The point which he
does not make plain is that the knights in Malta were in an even
more commanding position than they had been in Rhodes. There,
during the latter years, their efforts in the eternal war against the
Moslem had been to some extent neutralized by the very fact that
their island was so close to the shores of Turkey. But in Malta, that
minute island which commands the east–west trade route of the
Mediterranean, they proved an even greater irritant to the sultan. His
interests and his tributaries extended right along the North African
coast to the far Atlantic and the galleys of Malta were ideally situated
for disrupting the traffic of the Ottoman Empire. They were not
content even with staying in the central Mediterranean, but were
constantly making forays into the Aegean whence the sultan had
considered them banished so many years before.

All this Balbi tells us, and he makes it plain that the sultan's interest in Malta was dictated by his new awareness of that island's
strategic position. From Malta, as he said, the sultan envisaged the
day when 'The Grand Seignior, or his deputies, master of the whole
Mediterranean, may dictate laws, as universal lord, from that not
unpleasant rock, and look down upon his shipping at anchor in its
excellent harbour.' For the sultan saw that Malta was the key to the
Mediterranean – just as it proved to be yet again in the second World
War. From Malta it would be no great step to transport his armies to
the conquest of Sicily, and win for his empire and for the Moslem
faith that island which had been lost to them when the Normans
captured it from the Saracens in the eleventh century. But Sicily was
only a part of the sultan's grandiose plan. He was engaged on ex-

tending his conquests into Europe (where he had been turned back before the walls of Vienna in 1529), and it was on the dissident national states of Christian Europe that his attention was really centred.

If Malta could be taken, and its harbours used for the fleet that would then invade Sicily, Sultan Suleiman saw that he would be in a fair way to embark on the major land invasion of Italy. Like Churchill in 1943, the sultan envisaged striking at 'the soft under-belly of Europe'. At the same time he was in a position to throw his armies across Hungary and Austria. His plan was a simple but thoroughly efficient one – of effecting a pincer movement on Europe. The lynch-pin of the scheme was the small sandstone rock of Malta. So long as the knights and their galleys were there, his communications with North Africa were interrupted, and he had no chance of landing an invasion force on the shores of Sicily.

King Philip II of Spain was the only European ruler who was directly concerned in the siege of Malta. The island had been a Spanish gift to the Knights of St John, and if it fell it was the lands of the Spanish crown that would immediately suffer – firstly, Sicily, and then the Kingdom of Naples. Elizabeth I of England had little or no interest in the Catholic Order of St John (which had been disbanded in England by her father Henry VIII), although she was far too astute a ruler not to see the potential danger to Europe if the sultan achieved his object. 'If the Turks', she wrote, 'should prevail against the Isle of Malta, it is uncertain what further peril might follow to the rest of Christendom.' But the fact was that she was in no position politically, economically, or even on religious terms, to concern herself with the issue. The Emperor of Germany had his hands full with the Turkish threat to his land frontiers, and further-more – like the other European rulers – was not particularly concerned in pulling King Philip's chestnuts out of the fire. Francis I of France, for his part, was even allied to the sultan, a formal treaty having been signed between the two powers as long ago as 1536. It was true that the Order of St John was very largely manned by Frenchmen, but they were members of an international group, and their interests in no way reflected those of France.

The fact of the matter was that, by the mid-sixteenth century, the Order of St John of Jerusalem was something of an anachronism, though Balbi very naturally does not see that the Order was doomed. It is true that the Knights of Malta – as they became known after the siege – continued to exercise their sway over the island and the

waters of the Mediterranean until the late eighteenth century, but
their apogee had really been reached before they ever came to Malta.
In the new groupings of Europe, among the national states that
were now arising, there was no place for the old international Orders
which stemmed from the Crusades. The age of faith, though few
realized it, was over.

The Knights of St John were a foreign legion of militant Christians
dedicated to vows of chastity and obedience, and eternal war
against the Moslem. They have rightly been described as 'the most
remarkable body of religious warriors that the world has ever seen'.
At the same time, Gibbon's remark that 'The knights neglected to
live but were prepared to die, in the service of Christ' contains a
great deal of truth. Sir T. Zammit in his history of Malta observed
that 'By the time the knights came to Malta, the religious element in
their foundation had fallen into decay. Their monastic vows were
usually regarded as mere form, and they were remarkable for their
haughty bearing and worldly aspirations . . .'

The Order of St John of Jerusalem stemmed from a Benedictine
hospital which had been established in Jerusalem in the eleventh
century. The hospital was dedicated to the care and welfare of
Christian pilgrims to the holy city and had, accordingly, played an
important part during the Crusades. In the twelfth century, as a mark
of his favour and a sign of gratitude for the work of the hospital,
Pope Paschal II had taken the Order and its possessions under his
personal protection. By now the Order had founded many daughter-
houses and hospitals along the old pilgrim routes through Europe;
benefactors had enriched it, and the pope's protection established the
Order as one of the most powerful in Christendom.

It differed greatly from the two other most important Orders of
medieval Christendom, the Templars and the Teutonic Order.
These were primarily groups of militant Christians who were com-
mitted to fighting the heathen wherever they found them. The
Order of St John, on the other hand, was a nursing brotherhood,
and the building of hospitals and care of the sick were its main con-
cerns. It was only as a later, and secondary, part of their duties that
the Order undertook the protection of pilgrims on their way to and
from the holy places in Palestine. The Templars, the most pros-
perous and powerful of the three great Orders, had been suppressed
on the specious grounds of heresy and immorality early in the four-
teenth century. The Teutonic Order never really recovered from its
disastrous defeat by the Lithuanians and Poles at Tannenberg in

1410. By the sixteenth century only the Order of St John preserved into a Europe divided by nationalism something of the fire and united purpose of the crusaders. By this time, however, they had changed greatly from their earlier foundation; they had been hospitallers first and soldiers second; now they had become fighting seamen first, and hospitallers second. This great change had been occasioned by their expulsion from the Holy Land in 1291, after the fall of the last Christian strongholds in Palestine. They had emigrated first of all to Cyprus, and then in 1310 they had captured Rhodes and established themselves in that island.

It was from Rhodes, for over two centuries, that the Order of St John maintained a ceaseless war against the infidel. The Turk now became their prime enemy, and the knights – unable to prosecute the war on land as had their forebears – turned themselves into the finest fighting seamen that the Mediterranean had ever seen. Their hawk-like galleys haunted the shipping routes of the Ottoman Empire, while they put ashore commando-like raiding parties wherever they could on the Turkish coastline, and at the same time maintained fortified advance outposts on many of the other Dodecanese islands. During these centuries the Knights of St John erected the magnificent system of fortifications which still amaze the visitor to Rhodes. They also perfected the form and constitution of their Order, so that when they came to Malta in the sixteenth century they made little or no change in their arrangements, but immediately set themselves to repeat the pattern of life and service which they had evolved in Rhodes.

The Order was divided into five distinct groups, the most important of which was composed of the Military Knights, or Knights of Justice. These were the sons of the great houses of Europe – who may have taken their monastic vows lightly, but who were entirely dedicated to their eternal warfare against the Moslem enemy. Before a knight could be admitted to the Military Order it was necessary for him to prove noble birth on both sides of his family for at least four generations. (The German branch of the Order contributed to its own decline by insisting on at least eight generations.) No taint of common blood or suspicion of illegitimacy could, in these early days, pass the scrutiny of the Grand Master and his Council, who investigated the claims of all potential members of the Order. To be one of the Knights of St John was at this time to be a member of the most exclusive 'club' in Europe, but a 'club' where it was very much understood that rights and privileges were paid for by an understanding of the phrase *'Noblesse oblige'*. If the knights were accustomed to almost every prerogative, it was recognized that they in their turn must be ready at any moment to die for the Faith.

When a young knight joined the order as a novice he spent a year on probation, as it were, and was then expected to join the Convent for military service. In Rhodes, and later in Malta, this usually meant serving first as an officer in the galleys, a complete year of duty being termed a 'caravan'. Three years of caravan duty were followed by two years in the Convent. After this a knight became eligible for the higher posts in the Order – the Bailywicks, Commanderies, and Priories. Many of the knights, after completing their service, returned to their estates in Europe – although always on the understanding that if ever the Order was threatened they would leave everything and come to its defence. Some of the knights, of course, and Grand Master La Valette was one of these, never returned to their home countries but dedicated their entire lives to the service of the Order. Such men were the iron core of the Order, and it was they who perfected its military machinery and enabled it to survive even the onslaught of Sultan Sulieman in 1565.

The second division of the Order consisted of the Conventual Chaplains, who were all ecclesiastics, and whose service was mainly in the Hospital and the Conventual Church. The third were the serving brothers, who (like the chaplains) were not expected to be of noble, but only of 'respectable' birth. Their service was solely of a military nature. The fourth and fifth divisions of the Order were composed of Magistral Knights, and Knights of Grace, who were honorary knights nominated by the Grand Master and his Council.

The most interesting arrangement of the Order was its division into eight Langues, or Tongues, consisting of the eight European nationalities from whom most of its members were recruited. These were Auvergne, Provence, France, Aragon, Castile, England, Germany, and Italy. The *lingua franca* for knights and soldiers alike was French, and the French influence naturally predominated, owing to the fact that three out of the eight Langues stemmed from France. The Langue of England had almost ceased to exist by the time of the great siege of Malta, having been disestablished by Henry VIII in 1534.

At the head of the Order came the Grand Master – a knight who, after many years' service, had held nearly all the main positions in the Order, and had then been freely elected by the other knights. The instrument by which the Order was run, and over which the Grand Master presided, was the Supreme Council. This consisted of the

Bishop of the Order, the Piliers or Heads of each national Langue, the Priors, the Conventual Bailiffs, and the Knights Grand Cross. The latter were the senior and most distinguished knights of the various nationalities. The Council, to which there are a number of references in Balbi, combined the wisdom and experience of both sides of the Order – the temporal and the ecclesiastical, each of which proved a useful check upon the other. The Grand Master could, if necessary, override them both.

Such in essence was the constitution of the Order of St John as it had evolved during the centuries before the Order came to Malta. Suleiman the Magnificent, the same sultan who attacked them at Malta in 1565, had been responsible for driving the knights out of Rhodes forty-three years before in 1522. After an arduous and ter-rible siege, in the course of which the sultan is said to have lost ninety thousand men, he finally forced the knights to capitulate. So im-pressed had he been by their bravery and courage that he accorded them honourable terms. He is said to have remarked, as he watched the aged Grand Master Villiers de l'Isle Adam embarking: 'It is not without some pain that I compel this Christian at his age to leave his home.'

For eight years after their expulsion from Rhodes, the Order of St John was homeless, and it seemed at times as if, like the Templars and the Teutonic Order, it was destined to break up and disappear. But in 1530 Charles V of Spain presented the Order with its new home, giving them the Maltese archipelago 'in order that they may perform in peace the duties of their Religion for the benefit of the Christian community and employ their forces and arms against the perfidious enemies of the Holy Faith'. Charles V was not without some ulterior motive in thus giving to the Order (in return for the annual token payment of a falcon) these islands from his kingdom. He undoubtedly saw that the militant Order of St John would be an excellent outer bastion beyond his more important dominions, Sicily and the Kingdom of Naples – his judgement being proved quite accurate by the events of 1565. Along with the gift of the Maltese islands went the seaport of Tripoli on the North African coast – a Christian outpost on the 'Barbary Coast', and a place notoriously difficult to defend. The Order of St John, however, had no option but to accept Charles V's gift, for they had canvassed all the other rulers of Europe and had everywhere met with indifference, prevari-cation, or a blunt refusal when they came to ask for a new base and home.

In the autumn of 1530 the Order of St John, under its Grand Master Villiers de l'Isle Adam, sailed from Sicily to Malta to take up residence in the island which they were to make famous. It is said that, when they first saw the barren sun-dried archipelago, 'they wept, remembering Rhodes'. The inhabitants of the islands might equally have wept, if they had known what suffering the arrival of these knights was to bring upon them. The peasants, for their part, were probably indifferent to the fact that they were now under a new rulership, for their lives of backbreaking toil on an impoverished soil and under a harsh sun could hardly have been worse. Indeed, the arrival of the knights may even have benefited them, for the knights had money to spend, required servants, and before very long were bringing down soil from Sicily to improve the agriculture of Malta. The local aristocracy, however, felt rather differently. Mostly of Sicilian or Aragonese families, they viewed with some displeasure the arrival of these polyglot European nobles – who even had the arrogance to declare that they did not consider the Maltese aristocracy eligible for admission to the Order. Mdina, the old city in the centre of the island, was their home, and no doubt they were delighted when they discovered that the Knights of St John intended to settle down in the fishing village of Birgu, near the harbours of the eastern coast. They withdrew with dignity into their palaces in Mdina, and had as little contact with the newcomers as possible. When Sultan Suleiman finally besieged Malta there seems little doubt that the attitude of the old aristocracy towards the Order of St John was: 'They have sown the wind, let them reap the whirlwind!' It is for this reason that one finds no trace in Balbi's account of the names of the island nobility – the Inguanez, the Manducas, the Sciberras and others (descendants of all of whom survive in the island to this day). On the other hand, one does find a number of references to working-class Maltese or to merchants, vineyard-owners, and the like.

Perhaps one of the most surprising things about the whole story of the siege is the willingness with which the native Maltese fought against the Turks. By blood and by language they were more akin to the invaders than they were to these scions of European nobility who now ruled their island. It was their Faith alone which made them constant, for the Maltese were among the earliest Christians in Europe – having been converted by St Paul himself when he was shipwrecked on the island in A.D. 58. They had suffered immensely over the years from raiders and corsairs, and they saw, perhaps, that only by a successful defence could their island ever be freed from the

constant menace of the Moslems. All the same, the conduct of the
Maltese throughout the siege is irreproachable – never a single
deserter to the enemy, according to one authority; while we know
from Balbi, among others, that a number of European soldiers
deserted. Men like Bajada, some of whose exploits Balbi recounts,
would rightly be a credit to any nation. Later historians of the siege,
like Vertot, Boisgelin and others, were more concerned with the
aggrandizement of the Order of St John than with anything else.
For this reason, they tended to neglect the Maltese contribution to
the defence. When one realizes that for every single knight or serving
brother involved in the siege there were at least one hundred Maltese
(not counting the women and children), it is important that one
should see the relative contributions in perspective. This, to his great
credit, is something that Balbi always does. Perhaps because he was
no more than a private soldier, he does not forget the deeds and actions
of other men like himself, although at the same time he never omits
to mention the truly fantastic courage displayed by the knights.

The hero of his account is undoubtedly Grand Master La Valette,
and a more remarkable example of a man cast in the ancient heroic
mould scarcely ever existed. Born in 1494, Jean Parisot de la Valette
had joined the Order when he was twenty years old. He was
descended from a noble Provençal family which had already given
a number of knights to the Order, among his ancestors were
men who had fought in the Crusades with St Louis. A single-
minded and dedicated man if ever there was one, La Valette never
revisited his native France. From the day that he joined the Order of
St John his life was given over entirely to its service. Had there been
more Catholics like La Valette in the sixteenth century, it is more
than likely that the Counter-Reformation would have been wholly
successful. It was said of him that 'He was capable of converting a
Protestant or governing a kingdom.' The Abbé de Brantôme described him as 'A very handsome man, tall, calm and unemotional,
speaking several languages fluently – Italian, Spanish, Greek, Arabic
and Turkish.' This, then, was no simple sea-dog, no Christian
pirate, but something of an intellectual, yet an 'intellectual' who had
been raised in the hard trade of war and who accepted wholeheartedly
the Faith of the Catholic Church. He was an able politician and,
where the interests of his Order were concerned, was able to compete
with the keenest and most astute rulers of the time. After the siege,
when all Christendom united to do him honour, it is noteworthy
that La Valette graciously declined the cardinal's hat which Pope

Pius V sent to him. By some historians this action has been ascribed to a natural modesty in the Grand Master, but it seems far more likely that it was due to his political commonsense. As Grand Master of the Order of St John of Jerusalem, he enjoyed a cardinal's distinction, but without in any way being obligated to the Vatican. He saw rightly that for the health of the Order it was better for its Grand Master to retain as much liberty as possible from any outside interference.

La Valette had learned his Arabic and Turkish as a galley-slave. Captured in a sea-battle in 1541, he had suffered the inevitable fate that befell the losers in that day and age. For a year he toiled at the oar, until an exchange of prisoners between the corsairs of the North African coast and the Order of St John secured his release. To survive such an ordeal necessarily entailed a degree of physical fitness and endurance that it is hard for twentieth-century dwellers to comprehend. Life for all classes in the sixteenth century city was a question of the survival of the fittest. When one bears in mind that Grand Master La Valette was seventy years of age at the time of the siege of Malta, and that he was still capable of fighting in the breach in a mid-summer temperature of 100° or so, one has some conception of the degree of physical hardihood to which he had attained. When such iron endurance was coupled with a fanatical belief in the righteousness of one's Faith and cause, it can be seen that a struggle of this nature was harsh and bitter. For it was not only among the Christians that men of La Valette's calibre were to be found. Dragut, the Turkish corsair, was another man of similar mettle. He, too, had served his time as a galley-slave. Like La Valette, his whole life had been passed in warfare.

The Grand Master, during his long service with the Order of St John, had held almost all the important positions that were available. He had been Lieutenant to the previous Grand Master, General of the Fleet, and Governor of Tripoli. (When that North African city was lost in 1551, it was largely because La Valette's recommendations as to its security had not been followed.) He was the first General of the Fleet not to be of Italian blood – this position being normally considered an Italian sinecure. A born soldier, he had distinguished himself in each and every one of the positions that he had held, so it came as no great surprise when in 1557, on the death of Grand Master La Sengle, 'the universal voice was in favour of La Valette, under whose government the Order regained its ancient authority'. This quotation from a French historian of the

Order, J. Baudoin, reveals the fact that the Order had noticeably declined during the first half of the sixteenth century. To a certain extent this was due to maladministration; and one of the first things that La Valette took in hand, on becoming Grand Master, was the reorganization of the Order's finances. The disappearance of that 'rich, noble and important Langue', England, during the reign of Henry VIII, had been a setback. Then it became clear that a number of the more important German knights were not only loath to serve their time in Malta, but were omitting to pay their dues. Similar laxities throughout the whole of the Order's financial system were rapidly eliminated during the Grand Mastership of La Valette. He was not only a strategist, a tactician, and a dauntless soldier, but he was 'modern' enough in his outlook to know that any military organization needs a regular and adequate supply of funds in order to exist. Similarly, throughout the siege itself, his forethought and practicality were shown on innumerable occasions. As Balbi remarks: 'If it had not been for the constant foresight and preparations made by the Grand Master, not one of us would have survived . . .'

The main defences of Malta at the time of the siege were, firstly, Fort St Angelo at the end of the main peninsula on the southern side of Grand Harbour. This was separated by a narrow sea-filled ditch from the main base of the knights, the village (for it was no more) of Birgu. The whole of Birgu was walled round, and protected by the elaborate system of curtain walls and bastions which were a feature of defended places in the sixteenth century. It was, however, only a faint shadow of the elaborate fortifications which the knights had constructed to protect their city of Rhodes. In the thirty-five years that the Order had been in Malta they had done what they could to improve the defences of what was, to all effects, a totally undefended island when they came to it. But thirty-five years was little enough time in those days, coupled with the financial instability that followed the expulsion from Rhodes, to make Malta a really efficient base. La Valette, from the moment that he took charge, did what he could to improve the fortifications, and it is proof of his abilities in this direction that they stood up so well to the massive fire-power of the Turkish artillery.

The second main defence-point of the island was the peninsula of Senglea, so-called after Grand Master La Sengle who had founded the village upon it. This lay immediately next to the peninsula on which Birgu was situated, but was never so strongly protected. It lacked a fortress like St Angelo at its seamost end, and not enough time or money had been available to make it equivalently strong. It was on this peninsula, called throughout his account 'St Michael's', after its main defence-point, that Balbi served as an arquebusier during the siege.

The third fortress of the island, if such it could really be called, was the small star-shaped fort of St Elmo at the seaward extremity of Mount Sciberras, to the north of Grand Harbour. This was in no sense a walled and fortified township, but a small 'guard' fortress built to command the entrance to Grand Harbour on the one side, and Marsamuscetto harbour on the other. It had only been constructed in 1552 and, although it was built of sand-and-limestone blocks, it had been hastily erected, and was certainly no match for the efficient siege artillery employed by the Turks. It was upon the defence of St Elmo that, as it turned out, the whole safety of the island depended. The Turks, as we learn from Balbi, made the fantastic mistake of wasting their time in the siege of this fort, thus allowing the defenders to bring the two main positions into a state of complete readiness. It is noticeable that the corsair Dragut, the moment that he arrived upon the scene, pointed out the stupidity of ever having bothered with St Elmo. His assessment, and that of Mustapha Pasha, was quite correct – if the Turks had first taken the island from the north downwards, including the old and weakly-defended citadel of Mdina, they would never have needed to bother with Fort St Elmo. Having cut off the two main garrisons from any possibility of contact with Sicily, the Turkish army could no doubt have subdued them within the space of a few weeks. But, having made the mistake of attacking St Elmo first (in order to provide the Turkish fleet with a safe anchorage in Marsamuscetto), the Turkish command then made the further, and even worse mistake, of not seeing that St Elmo was cut off by sea, so that no reinforcements could reach it from St Angelo and Birgu. For almost a month La Valette was able to send a blood transfusion of men, stores, and ammunition every night into the beleaguered garrison.

The inadequacies of the Turkish Command are made very clear by Balbi, and the rivalry between the two pashas – Mustapha, pasha of the land forces, and Piali, pasha of the fleet – was the real rock upon which the whole Turkish campaign foundered. Both of them had proved themselves able men in many other campaigns by land and sea, but it was Sultan Suleiman's wish to have a double-headed command that really wrecked the expedition.

One of the points upon which Balbi is reticent is the late arrival of the main relief force, sent by Don Garcia de Toledo, Viceroy of Sicily. To all the later historians of the Order Don Garcia was the villain of the piece, and there was little bad enough that they could find to say about him. It is hardly surprising that Balbi avoids these dangerous political waters. He was, after all, no more than a humble arquebusier; his book was printed with the licence of His Most Catholic Majesty, Philip II of Spain; and King Philip was the man who had appointed Don Garcia, Viceroy of Sicily.

In a note to Balbi's manuscript (p. 162), I have suggested some of the reasons which may have prompted Don Garcia's reluctance to commit himself to relieving Malta – until such a moment as it seemed clear that the relief had every chance of success. The fact remains that he would seem to have incurred his Sovereign's displeasure for, soon after the siege was raised, Don Garcia passes into obscurity. One authority has it that La Valette complained to Philip II about his viceroy's behaviour. Certainly he had good reason to do so, for – as Balbi omits to mention – La Valette had been assured of relief on at least two occasions long before the end of July, let alone mid-September. Don Garcia, in any case, was relieved of the governor-ship of Sicily, retiring to Naples, 'where he passed the remainder of his days, without public employment of any kind, and died in obscurity'.

Balbi ends his account of the siege with a brief review of the events of the following year. He was naturally not in a position to assess exactly what the successful defence of Malta had achieved. It had, in fact, proved one of the most important single incidents in the history of the Wars of Religion. The blow suffered by the Turks in their failure at Malta was something from which they never quite recovered. It was not so much the loss of manpower – though that in itself was considerable – but it was the blow to prestige, and the 'loss of face' involved in the failure of their mighty fleet and army to take 'that obscure, sandstone rock', which acted as a demoralizing factor. Six years later, at the Battle of Lepanto, when the ships of the Christian league, aided and assisted by galleys sent by the Knights of Malta, defeated the Ottoman fleet, the real fruits of La Valette's defence of Malta were plainly visible. The myth of the omnipotent Ottoman fleet, and of those superhuman warriors, the Janissaries, had been exploded at Malta in 1565. This is not to deny that, for several centuries afterwards, the Ottoman Empire embraced a large section of Eastern Europe. But never again did the Turks make a major effort to break into the waters of the central or western Mediterranean. Occasional half-hearted attempts were made in later centuries to penetrate beyond the defences of Malta, but none of them came to anything. By that time Malta was, indeed, an almost impregnable island; and it was not until the changed conditions of warfare in the Napoleonic period, coupled with the demoralization of the Order of St John, that Malta fell – not to its ancient Moslem enemies, but to the forces of the French Revolution.

The news of the relief of Malta was carried all over Europe by eager messengers. From the cities of Sicily, to Rome, Paris, and even as far as London, church bells pealed out this great Christian success in the war against the infidel. Never again in history would there be quite such an occasion, and the bells which told the joyful news tolled, in effect, the death-knell of the old Christian solidarity (such as it had been), and the final demise of the spirit of the Crusades. While, for two centuries more, a polyglot, international Order contrived to rule Malta and to extend their power over Levantine and central Mediterranean seas, the rest of Christendom was to divide into those strong national groupings the problems of which still bedevil us.

W. H. Prescott in his *History of Philip II* wrote that 'The arms of Soleyman the First, during his long and glorious reign, met with no reverse so humiliating as his failure in the siege of Malta. To say nothing of the cost of the maritime preparations, the waste of life was prodigious . . .' On the estimate of the most conservative of historians, the Turks and their tributaries lost some twenty-five thousand men. Seeing that there were no records kept of the losses sustained by the corsairs and Barbary pirates who were also engaged in the expedition, it is probable that thirty thousand dead would be nearer the mark. Out of an original garrison force, which had totalled about nine thousand men, the Grand Master had only some six hundred left capable of bearing arms by the end of the siege. Out of five hundred and forty-one knights and men-at-arms who were in Malta at the beginning of the Turkish attack, two hundred and fifty were dead, and the remainder, almost without exception, were crippled for life. The island of Malta itself was a ruin and, as Vertot tells us, when the relief force looked around them, 'their hearts were filled with unspeakable anguish'.

Out of the tragedy, though, there sprang one of the most remarkable cities and systems of defensive constructions in the history of mankind. La Valette had not been slow to see the weakness of the present system of the island's defences. As Balbi makes quite clear, the major fault was that Forts St Elmo, St Angelo, Birgu, and St Michael's, were all dominated by different sections of higher ground. Some years before the siege, in fact, the two distinguished fortress-engineers, Count Strozzi and Antonio Ferramolino, had pointed out that the high land of Mount Sciberras – rising behind and above Fort St Elmo – was the ideal place for the knights' new home. It was here that La Valette, together with his architect and fortress-engineer Francesco Laparelli, decided to build the new base and citadel of the Order. Called after its most famous Grand Master, the city of Valetta saw its foundation stone laid on 28 March 1566, only six months after the siege had been raised. *Humillima Civitas Valettae*, the Most Humble City of Valetta, it was formally called, although it came to be known throughout Europe in later years as *Superbissima*, the Most Proud.

The future history of some of the main actors in the drama must not be forgotten. The sultan, Suleiman the Magnificent, whose immense shadow hangs over the whole scene, died the following year, while engaged on the siege of a city in Hungary. After his defeat in Malta he had intended, so historians tell us, to make a further attempt in person in 1566. For whatever reasons, most probably the immense expense involved in such a seaborne operation, he changed his mind and died as he had largely lived to the thunder of siege guns on a foreign battlefield. His two pashas, Mustapha and Piali, had been spared by his clemency upon their return from Malta. Mustapha

fades out of history, but the younger Piali went on to redeem himself
to some extent by successful operations against various Aegean islands. In the following year, 1566, he captured the island of Chios
from the Genoese. El Louck Ali, Governor of Alexandria, was one
of the only Turkish admirals to come successfully out of the battle of
Lepanto in 1571. An able tactician, he extricated his own squadron
from the collapse of the Turkish centre, having previously come near
to achieving victory for the Turks by driving in the whole of the
Christian right wing under its admiral, Andrea Doria.

Grand Master La Valette himself lived on for another three years.
They were not entirely happy years for, almost as soon as the Turkish
threat was withdrawn from Malta, the feuds, dissensions, and arguments over position and preference, which always bedevilled the
knights' relationships, quickly sprang up again. La Valette, however, could take comfort in the sight of his new city rising proud and
shining over the embattled heights of Mount Sciberras. To few men
is it given to see a dream coming to fruition in the declining years of
their life. After a stroke in July 1568, following a day spent out on
horseback, hawking under the harsh sun of midsummer Malta, he
lingered on for several weeks in his palace in Birgu, and died having
set his household slaves at liberty, and after adjuring his brethren to
live together in the same unity that they had displayed during the
siege. He was laid to rest in his new city of Valetta. His body now
lies in the crypt of the great cathedral of St John.

Of our historian we know only that the poor poet and historian,
Francisco Balbi, died in his 84th year. 'Ever persecuted by men and
by fortune', he resembles Cervantes in this, at least. It was, no doubt,
poverty that drove him to enlist in the ranks of the Spanish arquebusiers. He writes in a comparatively simple but unimaginative
Spanish, and if I have been guilty of liberties with his text, it has
mostly been in using synonyms for adjectives, verbs, and nouns,
which he tends to employ repetitiously. I have also omitted cata-
logues of names which can be of little interest to the general reader.
Francisco Balbi died 'away from his native land', but he has his
monument in his history of the great siege of Malta.

> 'Old men forget; yet all shall be forgot,
> But he'll remember with advantages
> What feats he did that day . . .'

Balbi lived to be an old man and, one hopes, had his share of
honour by some cottage hearth, or in some Spanish tavern. He did

more than that, for not only could he say 'I was there!', but he left for posterity his history of one of the great battles of the world.

To help to clarify the text a number of maps and plans have been included but it should be emphasized that in some cases the information given is inevitably hypothetical since no detailed records exist.

THE SIEGE OF MALTA

THE AUTHOR TO THE READER

AS in any book, and invariably in a first impression, it is natural to find errors owing to the author and the printer. It is not surprising, for many reasons, that my book is no exception. Consequently this second edition has been revised, corrected, amended, and considerably amplified without either changing my style or altering the truth. The alterations have been made at the suggestion of a number of Knights of the Order of St John, and of other Orders. Since this does not prejudice my history, but indeed adds to its interest, I have thought it fitting to concur with their suggestions. I have therefore incorporated some other details about various people who took part in the siege and in the Council. In general I have followed my original plan with all its known and agreed truth.

I

THE SULTAN SULEIMAN PREPARES
HIS EXPEDITION AGAINST THE
ISLAND OF MALTA

AFTER the death of Claude de la Sengle, Jean de la Valette was chosen as Grand Master of the Order of St John, and it is he who still holds this position. He is a French knight of the Langue of Provence, a very good Christian, and a soldier who is not only brave but wise, as well as being a great leader. Before he reached the highest rank of the Order, he held a number of varying positions, from being captain of a galley to being in charge of all the fleet. He had been Bailiff of Lango, Governor of Tripoli, and had also been present at the siege of Rhodes.

Jean de la Valette was elected Grand Master in August 1557. So that his qualities can be appreciated, I shall briefly describe his nature and his appearance for the benefit of those who have never seen or known him.

In the year 1565[1561] he was sixty-seven years old. Tall and very well built, his appearance is extremely dignified, and he has the manner of authority befitting a Grand Master. In temperament he is rather melancholy, but for his age he is very robust, as has been demonstrated in the siege. A very devout man, he has a good memory, wisdom and intelligence, and, from his experiences of warfare both on land and sea, has acquired an excellent judgement. Moderate in his actions, patient in difficulty, he is an accomplished linguist, but above all, he is a lover of justice, and enjoys the good opinion of all Christian princes. Certainly, there can be no doubt that it took a man of his wisdom and courage to be able to resist the onslaught of Suleiman which took place, as I shall now tell, in this year 1565.

It pleased God that this year, when the Order of St John was under the good governance of the brave and devout Grand Master Jean de la Valette, that Sultan Suleiman saw fit to attack the Order. Angered by the great harm inflicted on him by land and sea by the galleys and the knights of the Order, the sultan brought up an immense army

against them. He was incensed by the fact that in all the attacks made
upon his possessions in Africa, whether successful or not, by the
great King of Spain, Don Philip, as well as by his father, the
mighty Emperor Charles V, the galleys of the Order had invariably been present. They had taken part in the campaigns against
Tunis, Algiers, Galves, and at Peñon de la Gomera. Not content
with this, they had even attempted to capture various Turkish ports
in the Archipelago, such as Modon and the Island of Malvasia. All
this would seem enough reason for the sultan to undertake his expedition, yet it was believed in Malta that the real cause of Suleiman's
vast enterprise (commanded by his two ablest pashas) was something
quite different. I shall explain this by quoting the words of a Greek
knight who, on the orders of the Grand Master, was living in Constantinople at the time when the armada was being prepared. This
knight through his ability and knowledge of the language, was able
to penetrate into the chambers of the principal pashas themselves –
though at great risk to his own life.

Being at Constantinople on the orders of the Grand Master he
learned, so he said, of the sultan's anger against the Order of St
John, and of how it had increased since, in the early days of Jean
de la Valette's Grand Mastership, a most determined attempt had
been made by the knights to seize the island of Malvasia, an important strongpoint in the archipelago. The Grand Master, always
determined to inflict the greatest possible damage on the enemy of
the Christian Faith and of his Order, had hoped to capture the
island with only a few men and at no great cost. Malvasia had only
recently fallen within the power of the Turks – rather through the
treacherous conduct of certain ministers of the Venetian Republic,
and others in whom the Republic trusted, than due to any great feat
of arms on the part of the Turks. The Grand Master did not let the
matter rest, but immediately sent off two galleys, a galleot, and three
frigates; these he had been assured, would be enough for the operation. When the sultan learned of the expedition, he was as furious as
if he had in fact lost the island.

To add fuel to the flames, he then learned that Commander
Romegas, captain of the two galleys, had seized a merchantman off
the shores of Alexandria. This ship was on its way to Mecca, carrying a lady of high rank, who was taken prisoner along with the
others. It has been said that she was the aunt of Ali, the Chief Pasha,
but others maintained that she was the nurse of the sultan's favourite

wife. Whatever may be the truth of it, both these two influential figures in the Turkish court were continually urging the destruction of Malta upon the sultan. Gainsever was the name of this lady who was captured. She was over a hundred years old at the time, and was still a prisoner in Malta. Even worse than this, the same Commander Romegas, a few days afterwards, captured another ship in the same area, aboard which was the Sanjak of Alexandria. A man of the highest rank, and governor of a province, he was on his way, at the sultan's orders, to the court at Constantinople.

In the same year, 1564, five galleys of the Order, commanded by Pierre de Giou, a French knight, together with the two galleys of the Grand Master commanded by Romegas, captured a ship belonging to the Chief Aga. He was Master of the Grande Porte, one of the sultan's principal advisers, and one of the most important men in the whole of the Turkish Empire. The vessel was a very large merchantman, and was on her way to Venice, escorted by twenty galleys, when she encountered the seven galleys of St John. After a bloody battle with considerable losses on both sides, the merchantman was captured and taken back to Malta. It is estimated that this prize was worth more than eighty thousand ducats. As she was laden with silks from the Orient and valuable metals, as well as much other merchandise, it is not difficult to imagine the fury felt in the court of the sultan at the loss of so valuable and important a ship.

It is said also that the sultan's favourite wife, Roxellane, never ceased urging her husband to destroy Malta completely, and to this end she prevailed upon the imams to convince the sultan that this was the only way in which he could salve his conscience. The galleys of the Order were interfering with the pilgrimages of the faithful to the tomb of the Prophet Muhammad. On her death Roxellane left a large sum of money in trust to be devoted to an expedition against Malta, as a pious act for the repose of her soul.

When the news reached Constantinople, in October 1564, that Don Garcia de Toledo had seized Penon de Velez de la Gomera* – a fortified island and a haunt of pirates and corsairs which had long been a thorn in the side of the Christians – matters came to a head. This same year two letters written in Malta, one by the Sanjak of Alexandria and the other by the slaves held in Malta, reached Constantinople and came into the hands of Sultan Suleiman. They described the immense damage that the galleys of St John were inflicting on all the trade routes of the sultan's empire, and told also of the vast

* A harbour in Bodis Bay, North Morocco, facing the southern coast of Spain.

number of his subjects who were held in slavery in Malta, referring especially to the distinguished lady now held prisoner there. The letters declared that death was preferable to life in captivity, and indeed, they even reproached the sultan, that he, the greatest emperor on earth, should allow such a small island (weak at the moment, but which might become impregnable) to have the effrontery to oppose his might. Finally they begged him on their knees to take pity on his subjects in their desperate plight. A few days after receiving these letters, Suleiman summoned his pashas and ministers to a council. All these gathered in the presence of the sultan, eager to hear his command. Suleiman ordered the two letters to be read, and the recital aroused the deepest emotion in the hearts of those present. But by far the most moved was the Chief Aga, who had suffered more than any other at the hands of the Order's galleys, since it was he who held the contract for Turkish merchant shipping, and his losses had been very great indeed. In order to arouse the sultan even more in his project against the island of Malta, the aga spoke out as follows:

'Invincible and mighty Lord, if I thought it necessary to arouse Your Majesty by words, I would give you eloquent and weighty arguments. But I know well that nothing can turn you from your intention, or revoke the order that you have given in your wisdom, that we should utterly destroy this little island – which I am reluctant even to name. The thing that I regret deeply is that it should be at all necessary to send your invincible fleet and your mighty army against this accursed and insignificant island – just because nobody has bothered to take it for himself. It seems to me that we Turks who live under the invincible rule of the Ottoman dynasty are not like our fathers who served your fathers in the past, for they captured the whole of Syria from the Christians – and, one must admit, they are a warlike people. It was with equal courage that our fathers afterwards drove the Sofi into retreat in the mountains and conquered the Empire of Trebizond. In our own day, Your Majesty has humbled the ruler of Hungary, and made him pay for his effrontery with his kingdom and his life.

'Many other of Your Majesty's victories I could enumerate, but they are so famous that I will not weary you by speaking of them. I say only, that the people of this island of which we are talking shall have good reason to know the mighty power of Your Majesty, especially after the siege and capture of Rhodes which was much stronger and better fortified than Malta can possibly be at this moment. I conclude by most humbly begging Your Majesty to show pity upon your people, and to punish these knights without mercy, for they have shown no gratitude at all for the clemency with which Your Majesty has treated them on so many occasions. So that you may be confident of victory, let your army and your preparations be such that the pride of these men, who resisted for six months the great attack which you in person led against them in the island of Rhodes, will be abased.' With these words the aga concluded.

The sultan and all the members of his council were delighted with the Chief Aga's speech. It was again confirmed that they should carry out the enterprise, and for this purpose the various divisions of command were organized. After the sultan had listened to the advice of his council, he sent for Piali Pasha, his admiral of the fleet, and ordered him to get all the ships ready without delay. Both old and new were to be put into commission, and he was to build whatever others he thought fit. At the same time he was to muster all the trained oarsmen of the empire and to make all the necessary arrangements for provisioning and victualling the armada.

Piali wasted no time in obeying the sultan's orders. He summoned all the captains and officers of the fleet, to whom he passed on Suleiman's decrees. They were to make every preparation for the expedition at the greatest possible speed, and under pain of the sultan's displeasure. Piali also sent agents with his mandate to the coasts of Greece, to Anatolia, to the Morea and elsewhere, with orders to press-gang oarsmen. Furthermore he sent carpenters and shipwrights to the Black Sea (where wood is plentiful) with instructions to build twenty new galleys. As soon as Piali had given his orders, there was ceaseless activity in every shipyard, with new galleys being built and old ones renovated.

Before this, on the command of the sultan, they had also begun casting and founding heavy pieces of artillery. One of these was a basilisk of one hundred and eighty hundredweight, which fired a cast iron ball weighing one hundredweight. Two other guns fired eighty-pound shot and weighed one hundred and thirty hundredweight. There were four others firing sixty-pound cannon balls and weighing one hundred and ten hundredweight. For these new pieces of artillery, special carriages were constructed of great strength, running on iron axles and iron-rimmed wheels.

The sultan gave orders that six thousand of the best Janissary troops were to be selected for the expedition, and one of their agas was picked for the command – since the aga-general himself may never leave the sultan's side. Dispatches were sent to Greece, Anatolia, Caramania, and the Morea with orders for all the beys, their lieutenants and junior officers and all the fighting men under their command to stand to the alert. Mustapha Pasha was chosen to be captain-general of the army. He had been in command during the Hungarian war, and was an old man of great experience.

When all these preparations were well under way, the sultan ordered Ali Pasha to summon before him Mustapha and Piali, and he addressed them as follows:

'Do not think, my valiant captains, that what I am going to say is due to any lack of confidence in you. I know you to be two brave men, and I speak only because it is my honour and my reputation which are at stake. These are things which, in the battles and victories that you have fought under my banner, you have both clearly shown that you hold dear. But quite apart from all this, I have sent for you so that you could hear my commands from my own lips. These are, that it is my dearest wish to capture the island of Malta – not because it is important in itself, but because, if this expedition is successful, there will follow other more large-scale enterprises. It is to show you how serious I am, that I have recalled Mustapha from Hungary, where he was in a position of great importance, and have also given orders for all the forces in my pay to embark upon this expedition. I will now tell you why it is that I have chosen two of you to take charge of one expedition. One is to command the land forces, and the other the sea, a division of command I have never before practised. But so that you may fully understand my intention, listen to what I have to say.

'I have no fear of any of the Christian powers, but since you will be so near Sicily and Naples, which belong to the King of Spain, he may try to interfere with my plans by attacking you while you are engaged on the siege. This, then, is why I am sending the two of you, so that while one of you captures the island, the other may ensure that we have command of the sea. I am giving you both all the powers you need for the enterprise, and I ask, and indeed trust, that you will justify my faith and do your very best to be successful. If you do succeed, we shall try to accomplish what my father attempted – the conquest of Calabria, a task well begun by the capture of the important port of Otranto. Sometimes princes and rulers achieve success in unlooked-for ways. In our case, the capture of Malta would gain us considerable wealth and power, for we should then be able to send our fleet into the Western seas, and so enhance our reputation and damage our enemies. There would come a time when we should take that fertile land, Sicily, the granary of the Romans who once ruled where now – praise be to Allah and to His Prophet! – it is we who rule. Thus we should be able to make war upon Italy and upon Hungary, and the great German Empire would become ours. We should extend our sway to the limits of the known world, and your names would become immortal. On this expedition I am sending half of my children, the Janissaries. I know that they will be of the greatest help in gaining the victory I so much desire, and this is why I am depriving myself of my bodyguard. I have also allowed it to be rumoured that you are not only sailing against Malta, but against the whole of Italy. This is to keep our enemies in a state of uncertainty, and to make them divide their forces. Finally, under pain of my displeasure, I command you to work together in harmony in all things. If you do not, then all our labours will be in vain.'

When the sultan had finished speaking the pashas bowed their heads in sign of obedience and humility. Without a word they made obeisance, as is their custom, and departed.

Within forty-eight hours arrangements were made for collecting large numbers of hides, woollen sacks, old tents, and old sails for making defences and breastworks;* since it was known that in Malta they would find no material, and that there was very little earth. Vast quantities of powder and shot both for the artillery and for the small arms were also got ready. Lead, rope, spades, picks, shovels, iron bars, wood, and other materials were collected. All the artillery to be taken for the siege was examined and overhauled, including four reinforced cannon and four fearsome basilisks. To sum up, arrangements were made to take a great quantity of everything that might conceivably be necessary. Ten large ships were got ready, and were loaded with one hundred thousand iron cannon balls and fifteen thousand hundredweight of gunpowder, as well as a great number of wheels and carriages for the guns. Nine galleys of twenty-five benches a side were mustered, one of them loaded, after the utmost difficulty, with the great basilisk alone, together with its ammunition.†

---

* Important also for screening troop movements, since there was little, or no, natural cover in most of Malta.

† This was the one weighing 180 hundredweight. The 'four basilisks' mentioned just previously were the four described as weighing 110 hundredweight. The term 'basilisk' is loosely used by Balbi to describe any very large cannon.

Whilst the fleet was getting ready, the sultan ordered Dragut in Tripoli to prepare his fleet and join the expedition. A similar order was sent to Hassan, ruler of Algiers, telling him to alert all the corsairs in the Western seas. When at last everything was ready, they launched all the galleys, both old and new. The largest of these, with thirty-two benches of oars, was for Piali, the admiral, while another of twenty-eight benches was for Mustapha. So efficiently and swiftly had the preparations been carried out that the armada was ready by the end of February 1565. All that remained was for the galleys which were being built on the Black Sea to join them, but these were delayed due to the late arrival of their oarsmen.

At this time the sultan owned a personal State Barge, which was very richly decorated. It was quite small, having only twenty-six benches, but Suleiman gave orders that it too should join the expedition. On the day that it was launched there was great festivity and rejoicing both in Constantinople and in the fleet. The captain appointed to this royal command was a fine seaman and a descendant of Barbarossa, and known as Dali Suleiman. At this stage the galleys from the Black Sea arrived, but since time had been short, only thirteen of them and one galleot* had been completed. These ships and their oarsmen made up the full fleet, and the armada was now ready to set sail.

On the twenty-second of March 1565, Mustapha Pasha received the standard and the general's sword. He set sail with the whole fleet and army to the Seven Towers of Constantinople, the ships, the galleys, and all the other vessels bedecked with flags. They took their departure in an atmosphere of triumph, and to the sound of trumpets and the thunder of artillery from the castles which guard the Strait. So confident were they, and in such eagerness to be gone, that they failed to visit the tomb of Barbarossa – as was the usual custom.

The following ships sailed from Constantinople for Malta: one hundred and thirty royal galleys, thirty galleots, nine barges, ten large merchantmen, and about two hundred smaller transports.

The names of the principal commanders in the expedition against Malta were: Mustapha Pasha, Commander in Chief of the Army; Piali Pasha, Admiral of the Fleet; Dragut, King of Tripoli; Hassan, ruler of Algiers; the Aga of the Janissaries; and Cortucoli.

The admiral ordered all the ships to make for the nearest island for

---

* A galleot was propelled both by oars and sails, and was more of a merchantman than a strictly fighting vessel.

re-caulking.* Some went to Volo, others to the Negropont [Euboea], others to Chios, others to the Black Island, and the rest to the Island of the Jews. When the ships were all ready they reassembled in the port of Arnot, near Nauplia. While they were in the area, Ali Portu [the governor of Rhodes], Cortucoli, and the Caya Bey [Dragut's lieutenant] captured three ships from Ragusa which were laden with wheat and other provisions. These they commandeered for the fleet, paying both for the cargo and the vessels. The armada finally left harbour in a dead calm, the galleys taking the merchant-men, the barges, and the other ships in tow. But that very same night, while in the Nauplia Channel, although it was flat calm, one of the largest merchantmen was lost, together with all its ammunition and some seven hundred Spahis. Only the captain and twenty of the crew were saved. I am of the opinion that it was the captain himself who sank his ship in order to sabotage the expedition, for a great deal of ammunition was lost in this ship. While they were in these waters, two other ships ran aground, and would also have been lost if they had not been lightened by disembarking their troops and ammunition. Although they were very carefully salvaged, one of them leaked so badly that a great deal of gunpowder was ruined. Two of the divisional captains, together with seven other galleys, turned back to the port of Arnot where their ships were repaired and refitted. After this they sailed to rejoin the fleet, taking advantage of the good weather.

The whole armada assembled at Modon and in the excellent harbour of Navarino, for the fleet to revictual. While they were at anchor here, many corsairs from the Levant joined them. These were men who had been outlawed by the sultan, but were given a free pardon on condition that they joined the expedition against Malta. It was at Navarino that the pashas also mustered all their forces, the soldiers who had been conscripted for the expedition having come overland from Greece, Anatolia, Caramania, the Morea, and other parts of the empire, to assemble here for embarka-tion. There were a great many more troops than was necessary, so only the best were chosen. The least warlike, and others who had joined up unwillingly, were dismissed from the expedition – their officers making a great deal of money out of granting them their dis-charge. A rumour had got about in the army and the fleet that the expedition was likely to be difficult and dangerous, and that heavy

* The preparations had been carried out so rapidly that clearly the caulkers had not had time to do their job properly in the first place.

losses were expected. For this reason, those who were reluctant to join were more than eager to pay whatever they were asked, in order to secure their release. While they were in Navarino, the pashas treated the Janissaries and the Spahis to a number of banquets and gave them money and jewels. They were so elated by this that they felt that not only Malta, but indeed the whole of Italy was already theirs.

The total force which sailed for Malta consisted of:

Six thousand Spahis, all archers, commanded by a sanjak-bey and two lieutenants. These were the best troops selected out of the great number who had reported for duty.

Five hundred Spahis, under a sanjak-bey, from Caramania.

Four hundred Adventurers, under a sanjak-bey, from Mytilene.

Six thousand Janissaries of the sultan's bodyguard, under an aga, all musketeers.

Two thousand five hundred Spahis from Roumania.

Three thousand five hundred Adventurers, under the command of a sanjak-bey and an ali-bey.

Four thousand Adventurers, all religious fanatics. Most of these were men of private means, who were accustomed to spending their leisure hours in their mosques. Most of them were dressed in white, and some of them wore the green turban [showing that they had made the pilgrimage to Mecca]. These men had begged the sultan to allow them to go and fight for their faith, for they believed that their souls would be saved if they died in battle.

Six thousand corsairs and sailors, all armed differently.

In addition there were many Jewish merchants, who joined the expedition with a lavish supply of goods and money, so as to be able to purchase Christian slaves.

The total number of fighting-men who sailed from the Levant for the attack on Malta was twenty-eight thousand five hundred. A reliable estimate of the men who took part in the actual attack on Malta is forty-eight thousand. This includes the corsairs from the Levant, the followers of Dragut, King of Tripoli, and the force led by Hassan, ruler of Algiers. In charge of the artillery there was a Turkish General, and there were also five trained engineers, one Greek, one Slav, a Venetian, an Italian renegade, and a Turk.

Before they left Constantinople each of the Adventurers was given five gold sequins with which to buy himself arms and other necessities. This did not leave them much money for food, but many of them joined up in the hope that they would be rewarded for their services by being made Spahis. The oarsmen were paid two *aspers* a day (this is a silver Oriental coin equivalent to two or three *quartillos* in Castillian money). Before they sailed each of them was given twenty gold sequins, which was the sultan's payment for their services. Later on, many of these oarsmen took part in the land-fighting and also served as sappers. When the fleet originally sailed, it had provisions for six months, but this was greatly reduced owing to the loss of the large merchantman. Among the other artillery, Mustapha also brought from Gallipoli a large cannon which fired stone shot. This was one which had been used by the Sultan Suleiman in the siege of Rhodes.

On the twelfth of May, during the second watch of the night, the fleet sailed from Navarino. The weather was so good that it was off the Island of Malta six days later, on 18 May. It was first seen at dawn, thirty miles to the south-east of the island, with all its sails lowered.

Rumour has it that, when Malta was in sight, Mustapha Pasha produced a firman from the sultan which gave him powers over and above those of the admiral. The secrecy with which Mustapha had concealed this document from him, infuriated Piali. It is hardly surprising that from that moment onward there was little chance of harmony between them.

II

GRAND MASTER LA VALETTE LOOKS
TO THE DEFENCE OF THE ISLAND

THE preparations for so great an expedition did not fail to come to
the notice of the rulers of Christendom. Both through Venetian
agents and through those of the Grand Master, they were kept well
posted as to events. His Holiness, Pope Pius IV, and His Catholic
Majesty, Don Philip, King of Spain, were, in their turn, kept
informed by the Grand Master, for it was to them that he must look
for assistance if need be. La Valette did not fail to remind the pope
that he was the vicar on earth of Our Lord Jesus Christ, and Don
Philip that he held the special title of 'His Catholic Majesty'. He
reminded the king also, how important it was for his Kingdoms of
Naples, Sicily, and the Mediterranean Islands, and for his frontiers
in Africa, that Malta should not be taken.

When His Majesty knew for certain that the sultan was preparing
this armada, he appointed Don Garcia de Toledo, as Viceroy of
Sicily and Captain-General of the Mediterranean Sea, and ordered
him to make all necessary provisions for resisting the enemy and for
dispatching help as necessary. In February 1565, Don Garcia
arrived in Italy. Acting on the king's instructions, he held a con-
ference with the Duke of Savoy, the council of the Republic of
Genoa, the Duke of Florence, the pope, and the Viceroy of Naples.
After this he sailed for Sicily to take up his duties, and was received
with great enthusiasm. A few days later, having made arrangements
for the government of Sicily to be carried on in his absence, he
sailed for Malta and Gozo with three thousand Spanish troops and
thirty galleys.

Don Garcia stayed a day and a half in Malta, conferring with the
Grand Master, visiting the fortifications, and giving his advice. He
offered to leave some of his troops in Malta, but the Grand Master
said that until the enemy's intentions were better known, his own
forces would be adequate. He did, however, accept the viceroy's
offer to send an immediate relief force should it be required. Don
Garcia sailed from Malta to Gozo where he left what he considered
were sufficient troops for its defence, should it be attacked. These

consisted of four companies of Spanish infantry. He then returned to Sicily to make ready for anything that might befall.

When the news of the sultan's preparations became known to the Grand Master he immediately looked to the defence of the island, adding to the fortifications as far as he was able. The ravelin and the cavalier of Fort St Michael were very weak, so nearly all the slaves, as well as the Maltese inhabitants of Birgu, the villagers, the servants of the knights, the soldiers of the galleys, and the officers of Birgu, worked incessantly to strengthen them. At the same time the ravelin of Fort St Elmo was reinforced by an outer parapet of gabions and earth. Many of the houses of the district outside Birgu, which is known as Bormla, were demolished; these stood near the Post of Aragon and near St Michael.*

The Grand Master now summoned the knights who were in Italy. As a result of his forethought and preparations, Malta was now well prepared for the threatened invasion. On 7 May, the Grand Master ordered Don Francisco de Sanoguera to take out his galley, *St Gabriel*, and put in position the iron chain in place across the harbour mouth. Despite its great weight the work was carried out so efficiently that it was in position by 8 May. The same day, while Don Francisco de Sanoguera was aboard his galley in Marsamuscetto harbour, and his men were working on the ravelin of St Elmo, a friendly Moor (whose wife and son were living in Malta) arrived from the North African coast whither he had been sent as a spy by the Grand Master. He said that Amida, Bey of Tunis, had prepared a great store of provisions for the Turkish fleet, consisting of raisins, dates, honey, oil, and other things, but there was no bread since this was not available on the Barbary coast that year on account of the poor harvest. He reported also that Dragut, in order to secure the help of the Bey of Tunis, had sent him a present of many pieces of silk as well as some small pieces of bronze artillery.

The news that the Turkish fleet was at Modon was confirmed in Malta on 10 May, when Don Juan de Cardona, captain-general of the Sicilian galleys, arrived. Don Juan came with two galleys, bringing the troops of Captain Andres de Miranda, which were commanded during the captain's absence by his lieutenant Medrano, a very able young man of thirty.

Later on, Don Juan de Cardona came back again from Palermo where he had disembarked six companies of Spanish infantry.

* These were the houses of Maltese inhabitants which, as often happened in those days, were built outside the defences though abutting the main walls.

When he left Malta, he sailed all round the island, taking soundings
in the bays, and making a complete survey as he had been ordered.
He carried this out with the same efficiency as he always attended
to his king's instructions. Three days after this, two galleys of the
Order landed another company of Spanish soldiers. They were
commanded by Juan de la Cerda, and the Grand Master dispatched
them to the garrison of St Elmo, where they at once set to work on
the ravelin. Captain Fantone now arrived in another ship of the
Order, together with one hundred and fifty soldiers. These were sent
by Raphael Crescino, the Receiver of the Order at Messina,
together with ammunition, all at his own expense. Meantime in
Naples Commander Gil d'Andrada had arranged for Giorgio
Vercelli, the Receiver of the Order in that city, to enlist two hundred
infantrymen whom he put under the command of Hasdrubal de
Medici. Gil d'Andrada had them sent in the king's galleys to Sicily,
whence they were trans-shipped to Malta in the galleys belonging
to the Order.

Seeing that it was from Messina that he would look for relief, the
Grand Master realized how important it was to have a man of
authority in that city to deal with the Order's affairs. He chose
Signorino Gattinara, Prior of Messina, for this post, and gave him
command of the relief force that was being assembled. He also gave
him full authority to deal with all the Order's affairs, and authority
to borrow whatever money might be required. The Grand Master's
own galley had brought four hundred soldiers from Trapani to
Malta under the command of Colonel Mas, together with a good
store of wheat, and baskets for transporting earth. The Grand Master
now ordered the two knights, Luigi Balbiano and Adrian Maimon,
to get all the inhabitants and their cattle within the fortifications.*

All this time the galleys of the Order went back and forth
between Malta and Sicily. On the outward voyage they took with
them those who were useless for the defence of the island, and on
the return voyage they brought back provisions. Any ships they met
with in the channel, which had cargoes of wheat, wine, or other

---

* The inhabitants were, of course, brought in for their own safety, but it was equally
important that the besieged should have as much 'meat on the hoof' available as
possible, and not leave it for the Turks. At this point Balbi also lists the knights who
were deputed to see that the crops were harvested 'although they were not ripe'. In
the climate of Malta there are two annual harvests – spring and autumn. This would
have been the first spring crop, which would have been ripe in about another three
weeks.

A GENERAL VIEW OF THE SIEGE

a. Fort St Angelo: b. Birgu: c. Bormla: d. St Michael: e. Santa Margarita: f. The Belvedere: g. The Mandra: h. Corradino Heights: i. Boats being transported from Marsamuscetto: k. Two batteries bombarding Birgu: l. A battery bombarding St Angelo: m. Two batteries

bombarding St Elmo: n. St Elmo: o. Mount Calcara: p. Gallows Point: q. Manoel Island: r. Mount Salvador: s. Dragut Point: t. Marsamuscetto: v. Artillery being disembarked: x. The ford to Manoel Island: y. The chain sealing off Grand Harbour: z. Paulo Micho's vineyard.

foodstuffs, they brought back with them to Malta where they were well paid for their provisions. As for the Maltese who were sent to Sicily, Don Garcia had given orders that the Sicilians should look after them and treat them as good neighbours. Pierre de Giou, the French knight who was general of the galleys, and a devoted servant of the Order, was at this time on his way to the island from Messina. He met a ship at Reggio, with a cargo of wheat, whose Genoese captain, Geronimo Villavecchia, willingly sailed to Malta. Together with his men he served with honour right through the siege.

When everything was ready, the galleys brought over from Cape Passero cargoes of fascines for the fortifications of St Michael and St Elmo. Finally, Commander Romegas with the two galleys belonging to the Grand Master brought down to Malta three small ships laden with wheat. Their arrival was hailed with great joy because, there being a shortage in Sicily, Don Garcia was not able to supply the Grand Master with all the grain he needed. As the time for the invasion grew near, the Grand Master reviewed such forces as he had available. The following are their numbers:

Five hundred Knights of all the Langues.

Four hundred Spaniards under the command of Miranda and Juan de la Cerda.

Two hundred Italians under the command of Hasdrubal de Medici.

Four hundred Italians under Colonel Mas.

Two hundred Italians under De la Motte.

One hundred soldiers of the garrison of St Elmo.

Five hundred soldiers of the galleys.

One hundred servants of the Grand Master and of the knights.

Two hundred Greeks and Sicilians resident in Malta.

Five hundred galley slaves and mercenary oarsmen.

Three thousand Maltese out of the whole of the island.

The men, women, and children of the island were available for labour, together with a thousand slaves of the Order, and a great many beasts of burden.

There were three Royal Magistrates, Geronimo de Huete of the Spanish Langue, Balthasar Empador of the Italian Langue, and Antoine de Bourne of the French Langue. Apart from their judicial duties, they were in charge of the provisions and kept a muster of the labour force. They were also responsible for seeing that water was continually drawn from the Marsa to keep the cisterns of Birgu,

St Michael, and St Angelo always full. The water rationing was
entrusted to Commander Antonio Pacheco Caraveo and the knight
Marco Antonio Altavilla.

When the Turkish fleet was approaching the island, the Grand
Master called his Council. The dispositions were made so that each
Langue should go to its post (as is the Order's custom in time of
danger) to man the defences and to stand to arms.

*It is interesting to note that the Langue of England was only represented
by one knight, Sir Oliver Starkey. A close friend of the Grand Master, as
well as being his Latin secretary, Sir Oliver Starkey was put in command
of a composite force of Greeks and Maltese. The English Langue had been
disbanded by King Henry VIII.*

Between the fortress of St Angelo and the Post of England there
were two other posts. One was the prison, where the slaves were
kept. This was in the sole charge of the Governor and his assistants,
but it was more essential to keep a guard over the slaves than to
defend this post, for it was an extremely strong one, with two reinforced guns commanding the mouth of the harbour. Between St
Angelo and this prison, a fortification was prepared for the defence
of the harbour. It consisted of two heavy and two small guns
mounted on a platform. This position was manned by Commander
Romegas and the crew of his galley, and it proved most successful
against the enemy when they were engaged in the siege of St Elmo,
as well as during the attacks on the bastion of Castile. This post,
which became known as 'The Hub', needed few men to man it
since it too was very strong. Its defenders were, therefore, available
as reinforcements elsewhere in emergencies, as well as acting as
bodyguard to the Grand Master.

Below 'The Hub' and the rock on which St Angelo is built, at
the very tip of the peninsula beneath the castle, there was a platform
just above sea-level. This had a number of gun-ports and commanded the entrance to Grand Harbour, as well as covering the
chain which sealed off the entrance. The post was assigned by the
Grand Master to Commander Francisco de Guiral who, in company with his lieutenant Barientos and the men of his galley, *St
John*, fortified it very well. He had a deep communication-trench cut,
so that he and his men could enter the position without attracting
the fire from the Turkish guns mounted on St Elmo and the
Mandra. There is no doubt that this gun position saved the island,

for without it – as you shall hear – we should certainly have lost Malta.

The governor of St Angelo was Galçeran Ros, a Catalan knight, while Juan de Acuña was in charge of a reserve party of fifty men from the galleys. The Conventual Conservator was Juan Cortis, a Catalan, while Ramon Fortuyn, a most able executive, was in charge of the Treasury. He was a Mallorquin, as was also Gabriel Çeralta, a pious and dedicated knight who was head of the Hospital. Commander Antonio Flota de la Rocha had charge of the ammunition, Commander Pugiol of the artillery, while Commander Maymon, a Catalan, together with a Genoese knight, Salvago, looked after the gunpowder factory. They maintained the old stock of powder, as well as manufacturing nine hundredweight of new powder every day.

Additionally there were also relief parties, bands of Maltese troops and soldiers from the galleys who were kept as reserves, and only thrown into action at points where danger especially threatened.

St Michael, which was the Post of Italy, was commanded by the Admiral of the Order and held by the Italian knights. The admiral's command covered the whole of the peninsula of St Michael which was divided, on the Grand Master's orders, into separate posts under the knights who were captains of the galleys. The admiral's headquarters were in front of the tower, while the knights were stationed in houses near their individual posts. Inside the tower, which was guarded by knights, was a very large water-cistern as well as a good stock of ammunition. The Maltese defended a position from the water-point, near the Post of Aragon, up to the gate which opens on the trench. From this gate, up to the platform and casemates which guard the Post of Aragon, lay the command of Hasdrubal de Medici, assisted by a Florentine called Antonio Martello.

At the extreme end of the peninsula of St Michael there is a defence work called the Spur. Despite its importance it was not at all strong, being rather low, without a parapet or platform. The other end of the great chain, which closed the harbour, was secured to it. Francisco de Sanoguera, captain of the galley *St Gabriel*, a knight from Valencia, was in charge of this post. He was a small man, but of great courage and experience, and above all a very good Christian devoted to the Order. Don Jaime de Sanoguera, his nephew and a young man of great determination, was his lieutenant.

The Spur was fortified by Don Francisco and the crew of his galley as well as they could in the time available. Ably assisted by Vincenzo Cigala, Clerk of his galley, Nicolas Rodio, another clerk, Peri Juan Mendoça a Catalan brother, and Lorenzo Puche of Mallorca, he had a parapet and a fighting platform constructed, using four caissons of earth to achieve his purpose. They not only occupied themselves with this fortification, but took part in the fighting all around it.

The ancient capital of Malta (Mdina) was governed by Commander Pedro Mezquita, a Portuguese. He was also in charge of all of the rest of the island. The old city was reinforced, on the Grand Master's orders, by six knights and one hundred and fifty soldiers led by Juan Vañon. The Governor of Gozo was a Mallorquin knight called Juanoto Torrellas, the garrison of the fort consisting of eighty soldiers.

Luigi Broglia was in charge of Fort St Elmo. He was a Piedmontese knight, and had as his lieutenant Juan Giacomo Parpalla. The main garrison was composed of eighty soldiers under the command of Juan de la Cerda. A further fifty soldiers were sent to help them, as well as Juan de Guaras, the Bailiff of Negropont, who was also in charge of all the reserves. The cavalier was manned by knights, commanded by Geronimo Sagra and fifty soldiers. All the dependants of the Order were commanded to hold themselves ready, as is their duty, with their horses and arms. The Grand Master's Spanish secretary, Esteban de Claremont, was put in charge of them.

Throughout the siege, all civil and criminal actions were suspended by the Grand Master's orders. All civil prisoners were also freed so that they could take part in the defence. Despite the fact that commissioners had been appointed to ensure that the villagers brought all their cattle inside the fortifications, and despite orders and pleas on this score, the Maltese failed to do so. They thought perhaps that the enemy would do as they had done in 1551 – when they attacked Malta but left after capturing a number of the inhabitants of Gozo. The Grand Master had done everything that he could to bring the island to a state of readiness, but he was still uneasy about the impending danger. We, who were to endure the siege under his command, felt much the same as our noble commander.

III

THE TURKISH ARMADA REACHES MALTA AND THEIR FORCES ARE LANDED ON THE ISLAND

Friday, 18 May 1565. Our watchmen on St Angelo and St Elmo sighted the Turkish fleet thirty miles away to the south-east. As soon as it was seen, the pre-arranged signal was given for the inhabitants to take shelter inside the fortifications, and two guns were fired to warn Mdina and Gozo. Immediately, the islanders rushed to Birgu, bringing with them their children, their cattle, and their possessions. Not wishing all these refugees to enter Birgu, the Grand Master sent Commander Gabriel Gort to the gate of Aragon to divert some of them over to St Michael.

As the fleet neared the island, it was seen to be making for Marsa Xlokk. This is a large harbour five miles from Birgu, and safe in all winds except the Sirocco. When he saw their objective, the Grand Master dispatched the marshal from Birgu to oppose them with over a hundred knights, together with Captain Medrano's company and that of Colonel Mas, as well as some of La Motte's men. The cavalry under Captain Juan de Guaras went out with them – in all one thousand fighting men.

When the Turkish fleet was so close to the shore that they could see our troops, they realized that they could not make an unopposed landing, so with a fresh breeze in their sails, they took a southerly course along the island. Our men followed them on foot and on horseback until nightfall. Part of the fleet then dropped anchor at Mgarr and part in the channel. As soon as it was dark, sentries were posted at good look-out points, and our troops marched inland to Mdina to rest.

Saturday, 19 May. Before dawn the marshal set out from Mdina with the infantry, and went to Torre Falco, a high position from which he could see what the fleet was doing. Commander Guaras meanwhile took his cavalry two miles further on, to a place nearer the sea, and concealed his troops in a village. Not being able to see any of the enemy, he sent a French knight, La Rivière, a former page of the Grand Master, out on reconnaissance with twelve horsemen.* Their orders were to conceal themselves, and to try and capture a stray Turk so that he could be questioned. La Rivière was cautioned to be prudent, and not to show himself unless he saw his opportunity. If he should be attacked, he should stay where he was until aid reached him.

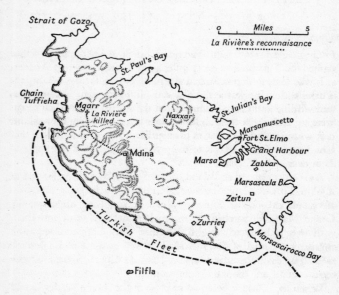

La Rivière did as he was told and was lying in ambush with his men, when a knight called Vendo de Mezquita, a nephew of the governor of Mdina, left the main body of the cavalry without any orders and galloped over to where La Rivière was hiding. La Rivière thought that he must have been sent to warn him of some ambush, so he came out of concealment and rode to meet him. Both of them were now seen by some Turks standing on a patch of high ground. Realizing that he had been discovered, La Rivière charged towards the Turks. Thereupon some of their arquebusiers opened fire on him and killed his horse. He defended himself on foot, but was wounded and captured. Vendo de Mezquita was

* Although the main body of the Turks had not yet landed, it is clear from what follows that small parties of them had already put ashore in boats to spy out the land.

mortally wounded, but, while the Turks were engaged in capturing La Rivière, he hid behind a wall, where he took off his armour and then died. His body and his armour were recovered some two or three days later, and he was buried in Mdina.

When La Rivière's horse collapsed a Maltese carried him about forty paces, but was forced to drop him and protect himself when the Turks attacked. As he did so he said to the knight 'Forgive me, Sir, but I can do no more.' This unhappy accident, brought about by Mezquita having acted without orders, greatly disturbed Captain Guaras, who now rejoined the marshal and told him what had happened.

In the meantime, a Neapolitan renegade had escaped from the Turkish fleet. He was asked about the Turkish plan of campaign, and what orders the pashas had given. He answered that their orders were to capture Malta and then Gozo, and that they thought the task would be easy because of their great numbers. He said that they had fifty thousand fighting men, provisions for six months, an immense quantity of ammunition, and many siege guns. He added, however, that the pashas were at loggerheads with each other, and that the Turks considered this to be a great misfortune. He told them also about the merchantman which had sunk, and of the distressing loss of their provisions.

Meanwhile the marshal and all his horsemen were in a quandary, not knowing what action to take. It was then that the knight Juan de Acuña, captain of the reserves in St Angelo, galloped up and told the marshal that La Valette ordered him to retreat immediately. His cavalry were to retire to Mdina, since this was the best place for horsemen, and from here they could do more damage to the enemy. The foot soldiers, on the other hand, were to make their way back to Birgu, for the Grand Master had been told that thirty galleys were hastily disembarking their troops at Marsa Xlokk in order to cut off the marshal's men. In obedience to these commands the troops retired to Birgu without any further losses.

The capture of La Rivière caused great sorrow to the Grand Master, not only because he was a good knight and one of his household, but because La Valette knew that the Turks would inflict a thousand tortures on him to get the information that they wanted. This, as we learned from some renegades, was what happened. They also told us that he said to his torturers: 'What good will it do you to torture me? You will learn nothing from me, except that you will never take Malta. It is both strong and well provisioned. More than that, it is defended by a commander, knights, and soldiers so valiant that they would rather die for their Faith and their Order (as is their duty) than show the slightest weakness.'

The same night the Grand Master sent Salvago, a Genoese knight, to Sicily to inform Don Garcia of the invasion. Only two days previously this knight had returned from another voyage, and throughout the siege he continued to serve the Order with great devotion and often at great risk to himself. No sooner had he reached Pozzallo than he handed over his dispatches and took ship again for Malta, as he had been ordered to do.

Sunday, 20 May. The Turks having thoroughly reconnoitred the island, now decided to land in force at Marsa Xlokk. Not fearing any opposition on a Sunday, they disembarked their troops in an orderly manner. Guards were mounted, advance sentries posted, and a fort guarding the mouth of the harbour was taken over and occupied. We, meanwhile, were busy working on the defences of St

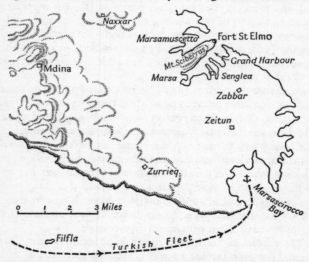

Michael and on improving the scarp of the ditch beyond the bastion of Provence – which was so low at one point that it presented no obstacle to the enemy. This same day the main part of the enemy camp was moved to the Marsa, the inlet where there is a spring which supplies drinking water not only to Birgu, but to any galleys anchored there, and to the other places near by. There is also a small hamlet close at hand, where the Grand Master has a pleasant house with a garden planted with large poplars. This attractive little valley is three miles from Birgu. The Turks chose it for their camp because of the fresh water, but before they were able to occupy it, a cavalry battle took place between them and the inhabitants of Birgu, supported by the troops of Juan de la Cerda in St Elmo.

The Turks now put a strong guard in the village of St John, which is half-way between the Marsa and Marsa Xlokk, and three miles distant from each of them. The object of placing this guard here was to give protection to their workmen and camp followers as they passed between the camp and the fleet with water and other provisions. Since their route took them within two miles of Birgu, they were frequently attacked by our cavalry, who often forced them to abandon their waterskins.

During the day the Grand Master gave orders for the houses which stood near the walls of the Post of Castile to be demolished, in order to clear the ground before fighting began. He also ordered the demolition of his stable which stood outside the walls, and had some pine trees cut down which were in the way. Soldiers, women, children, and animals were engaged in carrying earth from outside the walls into Birgu. This was piled in heaps, to serve for repairing the fortifications where and when required.

Monday, 21 May. The enemy had by now landed a great part of their artillery and ammunition. These they took to the village of St John, while their main base for stores and provisions was established in the Marsa. A well-ordered camp was now set up on the heights of Santa Margarita, and was bright with flags and banners. The sight of it aroused great wonder amongst us, as did the sound of all their musical instruments, for – as is their custom – they brought with them many bugles, trumpets, drums, bagpipes, and other strange instruments.

The Turks now made a large-scale demonstration in front of us, in order to reconnoitre Birgu and also to frighten us with their great numbers – for they were more than forty thousand. Realizing their intention, the Grand Master gave orders for all our drums to be beaten and for all our flags to be unfurled. When the moment seemed ripe, he sent out six or seven hundred arquebusiers under the marshal, Captain Medrano, Colonel Mas, Lamora, Pierre de Giou, Romegas, and many other knights. At the same time Captain Guaras charged out with the cavalry, and a fierce engagement took place. The advantage that the enemy had over us in numbers was cancelled out by our faster rate of fire, for the Turkish muskets are about nine palms long, and certainly not less than seven. The result was that they were not easy to aim and took a long time to load.*

The Grand Master held over one thousand men ready in reserve, he himself standing inside the gate with a lance in his hand to prevent the reserves from rushing into battle without orders. Had he not been there to hold them back, he would not have found a single man in Birgu, so great was their desire to get at the enemy.

This engagement lasted for five hours, at the end of which La Valette ordered his forces to retire. We did so well in this engagement that we killed more than one hundred Turks. Among them was a sanjak-bey, as well as other notables – or so we judged them to be from the care the Turks took to recover their bodies. The heads of many Turks were brought back into Birgu as well as one standard, which was captured by Monsieur de Prade and a Spanish soldier. We had ten killed, two of whom were knights. One of these knights was a Spaniard called Sésé,† who was distributing gunpowder to his men when a barrel exploded killing him and a further ten or twelve soldiers. The second knight was a Sicilian. Sésé had been in charge of the Post of Bormla, and the Grand Master now gave this command to Simon Melo, a knight of Portugal.

During the heat of battle, the Turks were able to reconnoitre Birgu from Mount Salvador and Calcara. Seeing this, from his position on the bastion of Auvergne, La Valette ordered his engineers to take appropriate counter-measures. Captain Guaras was wounded during this day's fighting and the command of the cavalry was accordingly entrusted to his equerry, Antonio Varese.

While all the fighting was going on, a Greek renegade, Baptist by name, escaped to the enemy. He was one of those who had been captured in the big Turkish merchantship.‡ Because he was circumcised [in accordance with the Moslem Faith which he had adopted] he had been put in irons. However, he was a first-class caulker and a magnificent underwater swimmer. The other Greeks had inter-

---

* But, as Balbi comments later on, they were considerably more accurate than the muskets of the defenders. It was the excellence of the Turkish marksmanship that contributed largely to the fall of Fort St Elmo.

† Here, as elsewhere, Balbi is meticulous in recording the names of Spanish knights or soldiers. As he himself served as an arquebusier in the Spanish contingent, it was natural that he should know their names better than the others and it must also be remembered that his account was written for a Spanish audience.

‡ The ship belonging to the Chief Aga, which was valued at more than eighty thousand ducats.

ceded for him, so the Grand Master had given him his freedom as well as a job as caulker in the galleys. Nevertheless, tempted by the devil, he left his wife and children, and went over to the Turks. Knowing how good a swimmer he was, the Grand Master was afraid that he might swim under water to the buoys which supported the great chain across the harbour, and drill holes in them. Accordingly he gave orders that four small boats should keep continual watch.

Tuesday, 22 May. The Turks again made a display of their strength as well as a reconnaissance in force, only this time in front of St Michael, rather than Birgu as on the previous day. At midnight the Grand Master dispatched the galley *Santiago* to Sicily under the command of his nephew, Commander Cornajon. This galley was chosen because she was the best and fastest out of the seven available and, to ensure her getting through at maximum speed, the headmen from the oar-benches of the other galleys were picked as crew. The knight Salvago went in the *Santiago* with dispatches for Don Garcia, as well as for Camillo de Medici telling them of the invasion. He was also to seek aid from his uncle, the pope.

A few days before the arrival of the Turkish fleet, La Valette had sent his own galley to the Barbary coast to gather news about the enemy's intentions. On her return to Malta, however, she was unable to enter the harbour because of the Turkish blockade.* The result was that this galley, as well as the *Santiago*, were forced to stay outside during the whole of the siege. This was the greatest of pities, for between them they carried six hundred men who would have been most useful in the defence of the island.

Having now carried out their reconnaissance of Birgu and St Michael, the Turks held a council to decide which place they should attack first. Mustapha Pasha, supported by most of the council, held that Mdina, Birgu, and St Michael should be bombarded simultaneously since there was sufficient artillery available. Mustapha told Admiral Piali that, in his opinion, Piali ought to go to Mdina with ten thousand men and ten guns, while he, for his part, would attend to the bombardment of Birgu and St Michael. They would thus achieve their object at one and the same time, and then be free to take Gozo, as the sultan had ordered them to do. If Mustapha's advice had been followed, we should certainly have been lost, for all our reliefs reached us by way of Mdina. But Almighty God did

* One of Piali's first actions, in accordance with his orders from the sultan, was to establish a blockade off the mouth of the Grand Harbour.

not permit that it should be so, for it was His will that the two Pashas in their jealousy should disagree violently with one another — as we learned from deserters.

When Mustapha proposed that Piali should attack Mdina, the latter was highly indignant. He felt deeply affronted that he, who two years before had captured the fort of Galves from the Christians, should not have been completely trusted by the sultan, and that Mustapha should be considered no equal commander to himself but his superior — as was made plain to him by all the Turks. Since he did not want Mustapha to be successful in any way, he spoke as follows: 'O Mustapha! On this expedition it is the sultan's orders that you should be in charge of all the land operations. According to their success or failure you shall gain either fame or dishonour, and no one shall share it with you. But just as you are in charge of the land operations, so it is I who have authority over everything in connexion with the sea. I am responsible to the sultan for his mighty fleet, which is naturally very dear to his heart. Now, if through my fault it should meet with disaster, the whole blame would be on my shoulders. If, on the other hand, it should meet with success the honour also would be mine alone. I tell you, then, that I will not be guilty of neglect, nor will I risk the high reputation I have fought so hard to earn, and perhaps even my head — as might well happen if the fleet met with disaster while I was away. What is more, the safety of the fleet was especially made my charge. My conclusion is that I shall not leave the fleet for a moment — at least until I have a better harbour for it than the present one.'

Piali's argument seemed sensible to the council, but Mustapha on the other hand, being the one principally concerned, did not agree. 'O Piali!' he said, 'I trusted in your good will towards me, but I see that I was mistaken. The time for dissimulation is over. I said what I did because I thought I could see victory for the sultan, and honour for us both if we had followed the plan I have outlined. But now you have raised the question of the fleet's security — and that in an island where even the inlets are harbours! However, I well understand your motives. I shall say no more except that I see us hazarding the whole success of this enterprise, losing many men, and wasting much ammunition. Worse still, we are likely to lose the sultan's favour, as well perhaps as our heads. However, I shall give you your safe harbour. It shall be Marsamuscetto — for it is clear to me that there is not a better one in the whole island, nor one more suitable for your purpose.'

The result of Piali's resolution was that the council decided to attack St Elmo first of all. Once this had been captured, the fleet would be able to enter the harbour [Marsamuscetto]. They hoped to be able to reduce the fort in ten or twelve days, or even less, and this was their first major error. Their second was in not waiting for the arrival of Dragut, although they had sent for him and promised not to undertake anything without him. They had assured him that his opinion would carry great weight in the council, but at the first opportunity they abandoned this consideration.

At the time when the Turks first came out into the field, the Grand Master, who was at the Post of Auvergne, noticed that they were paying particular attention to Birgu, especially near the Post of Castile – which was a weak point, with little room for the defenders to move. La Valette accordingly ordered that the houses in this part should be demolished at once. With the stones taken from them he began to build an inner wall, with plenty of traverses for guns as well as loopholes for the musketeers. The wall was so designed that, should the Post of Castile be lost, the enemy would find themselves faced with a second line of defence. Nevertheless, although the Grand Master had this inner wall constructed, he never for a moment thought of retreating behind it. He knew well enough the importance of maintaining the outer defence.

It was during this day that it became clear the enemy was going to attack St Elmo. As soon as night fell, they started to move their heavy guns to the Marsa, where they had set up their main ammunition dump. Mustapha Pasha now took up his quarters in the buildings attached to the Grand Master's garden. All this we learned later from a renegade who deserted to Birgu.

Balbi has no diary entry for Wednesday, 23 May, and it would seem clear that the events described above took place over two days. The importance of the decision taken by the council to attack St Elmo first cannot be over-emphasized. It was upon this that the whole success or failure of the expedition hinged. Mdina, the old capital city, was weakly fortified and held by comparatively few troops. The Turks would have taken it without any trouble, and would then have been in a position to cut the defenders' lines of communication from the north. This would have been disastrous for the besieged. They depended on keeping in contact with the relief force assembling in Sicily, and it was in the north of the island that the relief force ultimately landed – something they would have been unable to do if the Turks had been established there in force. Throughout the siege, the cavalry and troops in

Mdina also acted as a permanent irritant upon the Turkish flank, harassing their supply and foraging parties, and on one occasion at least inflicting really major damage on their base camp.

Thursday, 24 May. The governor of Mdina now sent Luca d'Armenia to Birgu to ask the Grand Master for reinforcements, and Vincenzo Anastasi was accordingly dispatched with sixty soldiers for the garrison. From the ramparts of the Posts of Auvergne and Provence we could clearly make out the galley-slaves and working parties transporting their stores from Marsa Xlokk to the Marsa. They made an incredible noise going back and forth, and our artillery got in some good practice on them, although they did their best to keep under cover. The Grand Master also had good news today from Don Garcia, namely that he was making haste to come to the relief of Malta.

The enemy, having taken the decision to attack St Elmo, now began to take up positions near the fort. St Elmo's garrison was eager to be out and at them, so Juan de la Cerda took some arquebusiers and made a sortie. This rapidly developed into a hot engagement, although the real aim had been only to let the Turks know that the garrison held men of spirit who were eager to defend their fortress. Now that he had appreciated the Turkish intentions, La Valette set free all the prisoners who were in chains, armed them and promised them liberal rewards if they would fight like good and brave Christians. They were assigned to the same division as the mercenary oarsmen. All the slaves, however, whether they belonged to the Order or to private individuals, were kept imprisoned. There were at least a thousand of them and whenever they were taken out to work on the defences they were chained together in pairs.

IV

THE ENEMY LAY SIEGE TO ST ELMO
AND DRAGUT JOINS THE TURKISH
FLEET

Friday, 25 May. The enemy now began to transport their main artillery from the fleet to St Elmo. This was a very difficult task, for the guns were heavy, their wheels and carriages were made of iron, and they had to take them a distance of nine miles over very rocky and stony ground. Unfortunately, the serfs and beasts of burden that the Maltese had left behind in the countryside proved of the greatest help. From the Spur of St Michael we could see ten or twelve oxen, as well as many men, harnessed to ropes, pulling the guns.

As soon as the Grand Master saw the Turkish artillery on its way towards St Elmo, he sent one hundred knights of all nationalities over to the fortress. Colonel Mas and La Motte, together with their men, were also sent to reinforce the garrison. Twelve galley-slaves from each of the five galleys were also sent over, and provided with arms and tools so that they could either fight or labour. They were given good pay for their part in the defence.

La Valette now gave orders that all the women, children, and old people who had taken shelter in the ditch around St Elmo, should be sent over to Birgu. Only men who were fit to fight or work were to be kept there. The result was that, when the Turks attacked the fort, there were eight hundred fighting men defending it. He provisioned the garrison with biscuits, wine, cheese, salt pork, vegetables, oil, and vinegar. As for fresh meat they had the island cattle which had been kept in the ditch around the fort. There was a fresh water pool near by but, since they would not be able to use it, the defenders threw salt into it. The Grand Master also sent over powder, lead, rope, combustibles, and explosive fireworks, as well as everything else that would be needed.

The 'combustibles and explosive fireworks' which Balbi mentions were to prove one of the Order's greatest assets in the defence of St Elmo, and indeed throughout the siege of Malta. Inflammable mixtures, known as wild-fire or Greek fire, had been used since the classical period in warfare. During the

Crusades the Christians in their castles in the Holy Land and elsewhere brought the art of making these ancestors of the modern flame-thrower or napalm bomb to a high degree of efficiency. The formulae for making wild-fire were closely guarded secrets of the time, but in essence wild-fire consisted of saltpetre, sulphur, pitch, resin, turpentine, and other inflammable substances. Sometimes the mixture was put into thin pots, which had fuses protruding from the end. These were thrown at the enemy rather like hand-grenades. In the defence of Malta, the Knights of St John also used a primitive type of flame-thrower known as a trump. This discharged a blazing liquid mixture upon the attackers as they swarmed up the walls. It sometimes had incorporated into it a device which fired a number of bullets. One most important invention that Balbi describes later was the firework 'hoop'. This was like a barrel-hoop, but covered with inflammable material. When thrown, or bowled down from the walls of the fortifications, it caused havoc among the Turkish troops in their long robes.

Saturday, 26 May. The enemy began to entrench themselves at little more than six hundred paces from the ditch surrounding St Elmo on the Marsamuscetto side. This was a very hard task, for the ground was all rock, yet they worked so well that before long they were close to the scarp of the ditch itself. On account of the direction from which they had approached, they could not be seen from St Elmo and so were unmolested. Soon their entrenchment was as usual decorated with flags. They also erected wooden triangular frames which they filled with earth, to form platforms and defences for the guns with which they intended to destroy St Elmo's walls on that side of the peninsula.

Juan de la Cerda now crossed over to Birgu and reported to the Grand Master. He told him that it was impossible to defend St Elmo because of its obvious weaknesses. La Valette thanked him for his information, but replied that he felt sure he and his men would do their duty. He added that he would send reinforcements whenever it was considered necessary. In order to put heart into him, the Grand Master said that when he thought the garrison of St Elmo could hold out no longer, he himself would come over with fresh troops and defend it. Soon after this, La Valette sent Captain Medrano with his company to supplement the garrison.*

* Balbi does not mention the fact that Juan de la Cerda was openly accused of cowardice, and that La Valette upbraided him for his lack of spirit. Either Balbi did not know this – it is mentioned by all the other commentators – or he avoided making any imputation against the honour of a Spaniard.

It was on this day that the Turks uncovered two gun platforms on the land above St Elmo. One of them faced the windmills on the peninsula of St Michael, opposite the Post of Don Francisco de Sanoguera, and the other faced St Angelo. It was clear that the first would be used to bombard the windmills* and the Spur, as well as the whole peninsula, while the other would command the sea-passage where the galleys and boats passed between Birgu and St Michael. Seeing the enemy's intentions, the Grand Master ordered the two galleys, the *Saint Gabriel* and *Corona*, to be scuttled. The other two galleys and the *St John* were safe in the ditch behind St Angelo.

Fort St Elmo, round which so much of the siege revolved, was a star-shaped fort which had been built in 1552. It had high limestone walls, and could not be undermined since it was built upon solid rock. It suffered, however,

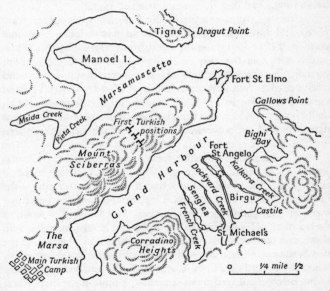

from the serious defect that it had been built in a hurry, and the stone used was not of the best quality. Also there had been no time to build necessary causeways, ditches, and subterranean tunnels, which normally enabled the defenders of a besieged fort to move about in some safety. Furthermore, like

* These were the windmills on the peninsula of St Michael which were used for grinding Malta's grain.

most of the fortifications of Malta at this period, it was built on rather low ground and was dominated by the high ground of Mount Sciberras.

The reason why La Valette ordered the two galleys to be scuttled was that they were lying in the stretch of water between St Angelo and the peninsula of St Michael, and were therefore sitting targets for the enemy. They were, in fact, raised again after the siege. The three galleys which Balbi mentions as being secure 'in the ditch of St Angelo', were moored in the narrow strip of water which at that time separated the fort from Birgu. St Angelo was connected with the town by a drawbridge.

Sunday, 27 May. The Calabrian renegade, Ochali Fartas, joined the Turkish fleet today, bringing with him four ships and six hundred Levantine troops. Also on this Sunday, Admiral Piali, while he was inspecting the trenches, was hit by a splinter of rock thrown up by a cannon ball, but the wound was not mortal.

The two gun platforms on Mount Sciberras were already completed, and during the night the Turks brought their siege guns into position. Before beginning the bombardment, the Turkish arquebusiers were told that they must all combine in a fusillade on our positions that night. Any man who was absent from his post would receive one hundred strokes on the belly.* They kept up this general fire for a very long time and, as soon as it was over, opened up with the heavy guns which had been trained on our positions. No great damage was done, however, for we were on the alert, having seen the Turks clearing away their gun-ports.

Most of this information I got from a young Spaniard, an Andalusian, called Alphonso. He was with the Turkish army and had taken part in this action. He was, furthermore, secretary to the Ruler of Algiers and tutor to his son. This night, during the bombardment, he managed to escape to St Elmo, for he wished to return to the true faith of his fathers. He put on his best clothes, as well as two shirts, and took with him all the money he could. As soon as the bombardment ceased, he made his way down to the sea-shore, where there was a cave from which the Turks used to fire upon our boats. Being challenged by their sentries, he told them that he was going to have a shot at the boats which were passing between Birgu and St Elmo. The sentries then asked him why he was wearing his burnous, and he answered that he intended to spend the night there, and sleep out in the open. He then fired several shots in the air (to

* The *bastinado* – caning on the soles of the feet or on the belly – was a normal Turkish punishment, as well as being used for torturing prisoners.

lull their suspicions) and immediately the chance presented itself, he went up to the walls of St Elmo and called out when he was near the drawbridge. An Italian sentry replied 'Che c'e?' ['What is it?'] Now it happens that this is also a Turkish phrase, so Alphonso suspected that the Turks had somehow got into St Elmo. Shortly afterwards, when our fire had died down (for we returned the Turkish fire), two knights saw him and asked him who he was and what he wanted. 'I am a Spaniard', he replied, 'and I want to come into the fort.' The two knights went off and told the Bailiff of Negropont. It was thought dangerous to lower the drawbridge at such a time, so a rope was thrown over the wall for him to climb up into the fort. Alphonso tied his arquebus, his burnous, and other belongings to the rope which was then hauled up, and afterwards he climbed up the rope himself.

It was from Alphonso that we learned about the quarrel between the two pashas, Mustapha and Piali, and of discontent throughout the army and the fleet. We also found out from him that next morning the Turks intended to destroy our big culverin, which was mounted on the tower. They would be able to do so quite easily, he said, for they had a Genoese renegade among them, who was a master gunner. Alphonso advised us to move the culverin before this should happen.

Alphonso was now sent to see the Grand Master in Birgu, where he repeated everything that he had told the Bailiff. He went on to say that, if La Valette thought fit, he would return to the Turkish camp at once and set fire to a large ammunition dump whose whereabouts he knew, saying that it would be quite simple to do. La Valette would not give him permission to go at the time, but the following night he asked Alphonso if he still wanted to put his plan into action. The Spaniard replied that it was then too late, for he would have been marked as absent by this time, and would certainly be killed if he went back. The Grand Master was pleased at his reply, because he knew now that he was an honest man. This same Alphonso fought well throughout the siege and was wounded during the battles for St Michael and Castile. After all was over, La Valette kept him in his service, employing him as a Turkish and Moorish interpreter, since he wrote and spoke both of these languages very well.

The story of Alphonso reveals a weakness in the Turkish system which caused them a great deal of trouble throughout the siege. Since so many of the countries in the Ottoman Empire were Christian by origin, and since so many Christians were employed, not only as slaves, but in other capacities and in all branches of the Turkish services, it was inevitable that, given the opportunity, many of them would desert. Many Christians who were captured during the course of their campaigns by the Turks somewhat naturally embraced the Moslem faith in order to save their lives. But when they had a chance to return to their faith and to their European brethren they naturally did so. To a lesser degree, the Knights of St John suffered from the same problem, for they had Moslem slaves, as well as servants from the Levant and other Oriental countries.

Monday, 28 May. The Turks now opened fire on St Elmo from the platform which they had built on the Marsamuscetto side of the peninsula. From one of the two platforms on the heights above St Elmo they also opened fire on the post held by Don Francisco de Sanoguera, as well as on the windmills, the houses, and the boats. From the other gun platform they started to bombard the battery of Francisco de Guiral – the one sited near the great chain. But, seeing that their fire was without effect, they turned their attention to St Angelo. De Guiral's battery being at water-level, they hoped that they could make the rock and stone above his post fall down and crush it. But as soon as any debris fell Commander de Guiral had it rapidly cleared away. Since the wall above him was very old, a great deal of it did, in fact, collapse. This greatly encouraged the Turks, but they would have had to knock down about thirty arms-lengths of rock before they could have done any real damage.

All the dogs in the island had been brought into Birgu and St Michael, and their continual barking during the night disturbed the sentries. For this reason, as well as to prevent their owners sharing their rations with them, the Grand Master had them all destroyed.* Meanwhile, the work on our defences went steadily ahead, the engineers building a parapet from the Post of Aragon to Bormla, which they knew was a weak point. The inner side of this parapet was filled with earth, but where it was too close to the main wall, it was cut away. Gabriel Gort, a Catalan knight, who is now Commander of Tortosa, was in charge of this post. Throughout the siege, as well as on other occasions, he has always been a staunch defender of the Order.

We noticed that the Turks were building a very large gun platform on the high ground above St Elmo, and it seemed clear that

* It is recorded elsewhere that La Valette also had his own hunting dogs put down.

this was designed for bombarding the fort, even though it was over a thousand paces away. At the same time they were steadily improving their position on the counterscarp of the ditch, which they trimmed down so that its height should not interfere with their gunnery. Throughout this period, the Grand Master never slept. He was like another Argus with a hundred eyes, inspecting, supervising, and giving advice wherever necessary. The moment he saw the large gun platform that the Turks were preparing, he gave orders that some small houses in St Angelo, which stood opposite to it, should be demolished. He then ordered a battery to be mounted at this point where the houses had stood, with the intention of bombarding the Turks from it. This new battery on St Angelo would certainly have interfered with the construction of their gun platform if it could have been made ready in time. Unfortunately, despite the Grand Master's efforts the Turks were ready before us. This was due to the fact that they had so large a labour force, as well as the great number of beasts of burden that the Maltese had left out in the country. Another reason for the Turkish efficiency and speed was that they had brought the materials and components for their gun batteries ready-made from Constantinople.

Nevertheless La Valette pressed ahead with the work and, as soon as it was finished, had four cannons mounted on it. With these he inflicted considerable damage on the enemy, and if only he had had enough ammunition, it is very likely that the Turks would not have been able to build their gun platforms as easily as they did. The Grand Master had plenty of artillery, both from the galleys and the other ships, but he did not have sufficient gunpowder, and was therefore obliged to husband his resources for the moment when the main attacks should begin.

Tuesday, 29 May. The enemy's main fire was directed against the defences of St Elmo, especially the tower held by Commander Sagra. The windmills of St Michael were the target for the new batteries on the promontory of St Elmo, as were the boats passing between Birgu and St Angelo. The Turks also bombarded the houses at the same time as they busied themselves on their big main gun platform. So well prepared were they for all eventualities that, even when some of their guns were put out of action by the fire from St Elmo, it was not long before they had them going again.

Wednesday, 30 May. The Turkish fleet sailed from Marsa Xlokk to take on water in the bays of Salina and St Paul. As they passed in front of Fort St Elmo each galley fired two rounds, and some of

them more. Their fire was returned by St Angelo and St Elmo, and
one of the galleys, which had gone too close to St Elmo, was hit
between wind and water. If the others had not gone to her assistance
she would have sunk. At the same time the fleet towed a number
of barges laden with fascines (for making defences) and other
materials into St George's Bay, and left them there. The idea was
that their barges would be able to coast round quietly by night into
Marsamuscetto Harbour and unload by their camp on the shore.
This was within range of Birgu and St Angelo and, if the culverin
on the tower commanded by Sagra could have been used, it would
have done them great harm. Unfortunately, this was impossible
because of the tower's weakness, so the cannon was removed before
the Turks could destroy it.

The enemy finished their large gun platform today and withdrew
from their positions facing St Michael. Already some of their guns
were in position on the main platform, and during the night all the
others were brought up. There were seventeen of them in all and,
judging by the noise they made, they were heavy pieces.

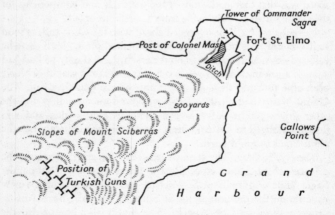

Thursday, 31 May. On this day, the Feast of the Ascension of Our
Lord, the Turks opened fire from their main battery, as well as with
the guns they had withdrawn from their position facing St Michael.
There were now twenty-four guns altogether in action against Fort
St Elmo. Some bombarded the post of Colonel Mas, the area
between the Spur on the Marsamuscetto side, and the other Spur
near the Church. Others engaged Commander Sagra's tower,

reckoning to do a great deal of damage. The commander, and his knights and soldiers, did all they could to strengthen the tower, as well as repairing it where necessary.

The Grand Master sent a succession of boats across so as to keep himself informed of the situation up to the minute, as well as to provide whatever was needed for the defence. Whenever they were able to open fire the garrison of St Elmo did their utmost against the enemy and, when they could no longer work their guns, they busied themselves on the defences.

Friday, 1 June. The enemy bombardment continued. It was as heavy as on the previous day and, indeed, so unceasing was their fire that it was clear they never cleaned their guns, or allowed them to cool in the normal manner. They relied no doubt on the great weight of their fire-power and, throughout the bombardment, La Valette was kept constantly informed of the effect it was having.

During this stage of the siege, work went on night and day in Birgu and St Michael. The captain of each position made whatever improvements were necessary to his fortifications. Some were raising walls, others building parapets and fighting-positions, while yet others were either raising the ground-level with barrels of earth, or levelling it off – whichever was necessary.

Saturday, 2 June. Dragut joined the Turkish fleet. He came with thirteen galleys and two galleots of his own, as well as about thirty ships belonging to other corsairs. Some two thousand five hundred volunteers from the western shores of North Africa were in this fleet, and Admiral Piali went out in his galley to meet them. He led them into St George's Bay where Dragut set up his headquarters before going on to meet Mustapha Pasha.

The Turks were naturally overjoyed by the arrival of Dragut, but later we learned that Dragut himself was infuriated when he found out that the bombardment of St Elmo had already begun. His own views were similar to Mustapha's, and had he been present at the great Council, they would have triumphed – which would have been disastrous for us. However, accepting the fact that the attack was already in progress, Dragut at once made suggestions for improving it – as was only to be expected from so experienced a warrior, and a corsair of his calibre. His intervention proved greatly to our detriment.

Dragut Rais, or Torghoud to render his Turkish name more accurately, was one of the greatest corsairs in the history of the Mediterranean. Born in

1485, he was eighty years old when he came to Malta for the siege. He had been a lieutenant under the famous Barbarossa and, on the latter's death, Dragut became the uncrowned king of the Mediterranean. He was known to his fellow Moslems as 'The Drawn Sword of Islam'. Although in his earlier career he had been at variance with the Sultan Suleiman, the latter had recently recognized Dragut's abilities by confirming him Governor of Tripoli. He knew the Maltese archipelago very well, having raided both islands on several occasions. Among his many successes against the Christians was his capture of Bastia in Corsica (when he had carried off seven thousand captives) and of Reggio in Italy (when he enslaved the whole population of the city). It was Dragut who had captured Tripoli from the Knights of St John in 1551. An old adversary of La Valette, he was undoubtedly the most able of all the Turkish leaders. He was described by a French admiral as 'A living chart of the Mediterranean, skilful enough on land to be compared to the finest generals of the time. No one was more worthy than he to bear the name of king.'

Sunday, 3 June. Dragut returned to his galleys which were lying in St George's Bay, to the west of St Elmo, and on the other side of Marsamuscetto he began to build a gun platform on a high point known as the Hermitage of St Mary. Although this new battery was six hundred paces away, he started to bombard the ravelin and the tower of Sagra from it. Astute and shrewd as always, he kept a good look-out so as not to be taken by surprise, and every night withdrew his men to his ships.

It was during this day, the feast of St Elmo, that the Turks captured the ravelin. Even the knights who were in St Elmo's garrison do not quite know how it happened, but the general opinion is that it occurred as follows. All night long the bombardment had continued and, even though their trenches were very close to the ravelin, the Turks had not suffered any casualties from the defenders' fire. It is likely, therefore, that their engineers went out along the ditch to see what effect their bombardment was having. (They could not go along the shoulder of the fortification, even though given continuous covering fire by their arquebusiers.) Now, to their great amazement, these engineers got quite close to the ravelin without being discovered. Going on still further, it seems likely that they either found the sentry asleep, or saw that the ravelin was only defended by a few soldiers. Thereupon, they gave a signal to the Janissaries, who made so sudden an attack that the guard was taken by surprise. They withdrew in confusion to a trench which lay between the tower and the ravelin. Now this trench was held by fifty soldiers, who had been posted there to give help to the defenders should they need it. Yet so fierce was the Turkish assault that our men were forced to abandon the whole of the ravelin. The Turks stormed into it in great numbers through one of the embrasures, while the defenders retreated into the fort.

This action was marked by great bravery on both sides. Many knights and soldiers rushed out from Fort St Elmo, led by the

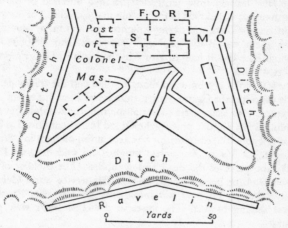

Bailiff of Negropont, to defend the ravelin, but they found it heavily occupied, since the Turks had already captured the trench. The Turkish numbers increased steadily as they fought to hold the ground that they had gained, while our men strove to regain what they had lost. A bitter fight ensued which was more than a brief engagement; it was a real battle, and the hand-to-hand fighting went on for five hours. In the end, however, our troops were forced to retire, for the whole Turkish army was coming up. They were sure that this was the day when they were destined to capture St Elmo.

It speaks greatly for the bravery of our troops that the Turks did not succeed. Indeed, during the confused fighting, some of the knights who were in the battle admit that as they re-entered St Elmo, they forgot to pull up the drawbridge behind them.

It had long been clear that the ravelin could not really be defended (although its exterior defence had been completed on the lines ordered by La Valette), and Juan de la Cerda had already given it as his opinion that it ought to be mined so that the Turks would be blown up when they captured it. All the same, the Turks did not capture it easily or quickly. After they had occupied the ravelin, they moved into the ditch in a confused mass through a breach in the outer defences. Our troops immediately opened fire on them from St Elmo and the tower of Sagra. If St Elmo had been built with embrasures for traversing fire, few Turks who entered the ditch would have escaped.

We later learned from renegades that five hundred of the best Turkish troops were killed in the assault on the ravelin. For our part, we lost sixty soldiers and twenty knights, and had many wounded, among them the Bailiff of Negropont and Don Francisco de Guevara. The Bailiff had an arrow in the leg, and Don Francisco a bullet wound.

The loss of the ravelin, even though it had cost the enemy dearly, greatly distressed the Grand Master, since it had been due to our own negligence. Our boats were soon transporting the wounded over to the infirmary in Birgu, a practice the Grand Master continued as long as was possible. But the garrison was kept at full strength for, during the night, La Valette dispatched knights and soldiers to St Elmo to take the place of the dead and wounded. The luckiest of the coxswains of the boats engaged on this ferry service was a Genoese called Arbenga, his boat sustaining only one casualty, Pagao, a Maltese serving brother. The losses in the other boats were considerable.

The night following their capture of the ravelin, the Turks began to increase its height with goatskins packed with earth. It was not long before they had raised it to the same height as the walls of St Elmo, even though our troops sallied out by the ditch and seized some of the skins. On this same night the Chevalier Salvago reached Malta and landed at St Elmo.* He and Captain Andres de Miranda inspected the fort together, before going over to Birgu. They crossed before dawn, under fire from the enemy trenches, one of their boat's crew being killed. Next day La Valette sent Salvago back again to

---

* Salvago had gone up to Sicily in the galley *Santiago* on 22 May with dispatches for Don Garcia. He landed at St Elmo in a small boat while the *Santiago* lay off to seaward. As we learn a few lines later, he was sent back – again by boat at night – to rejoin the *Santiago* and take further dispatches to Sicily. Piali's blockade does not seem to have been very effective, at any rate during the hours of darkness, and it seems more than likely that the Turkish galleys tended to follow an old Mediterranean habit and drop anchor in some convenient place overnight.

Sicily with news of the loss of the ravelin. He instructed him to make arrangements for sending a relief force.

Throughout this period there were constant skirmishes between the enemy and the cavalry based on Mdina. Our cavalry was composed of knights, foreign troops, and Maltese. On one occasion Captain Guaras (who was now recovered), having located an enemy foraging-party in a village called Mosta, went out with sixty horsemen and a number of arquebusiers. Falling upon the Turks, he captured some and killed others, cutting off their heads and sending them to Mdina. On another occasion, learning that the Turks were carrying off a great deal of livestock and corn,* he sallied out with eighty horsemen and forty arquebusiers to protect the Maltese who were bringing their corn into the city. Having sent a dispatch to the governor for reinforcements, Captain Guaras set off towards the villages of Mosta and Naxxar, in the direction of the enemy. The Turks, who were in a position of advantage, charged our cavalry, but at this moment the knight Juan Vañon arrived with eighty arquebusiers sent by the governor. Guaras accordingly determined to attack the enemy on both flanks. This move was so successful that the Turks were forced to abandon their booty and retreat in disorder, losing over eighty men in wounded and prisoners. Guaras fought extremely bravely, but received an arrow wound in the hand while holding his lance. Vañon also acquitted himself well, as did Vincenzo Ventura. The latter was in command of twenty-five arquebusiers and managed to capture a Turkish standard. In this engagement our losses were five dead and thirty wounded.

Balbi now lists a number of knights, Maltese, and others who distinguished themselves in this action. Among them he names a Maltese 'called Luqa, who had a strange method of capturing Turks alive. He had such dexterity with his sword that he would make a feint at the enemy, and then disarm them without wounding them. In this way he managed to capture a number of slaves.' Luqa Briffa, like the other Maltese hero Toni Bajada, is still remembered in the island and is the subject of many a legend.

* Despite La Valette's precautions, the Maltese peasantry would appear to have left a lot of their cattle at large in the island, as well as leaving the crops which they had not had time to harvest.

V

DESPITE CONTINUAL BOMBARDMENTS
ST ELMO CONTINUES TO HOLD OUT

Monday, 4 June. The Grand Master sent Captain Miranda over to St Elmo, not in a position of command but as an ordinary soldier (so that he could better judge what needed to be done), and he was received by the garrison with great enthusiasm. As soon as Captain Miranda reached St Elmo he found out how the morale of the commanders stood and what strategy the Turks were adopting. He inspected the gun batteries and gave whatever orders seemed necessary for the common good; his reputation was such that he was implicitly obeyed. Returning to Birgu, Miranda reported to the Grand Master. He stated that the fort could not be held for long if the Turks were persistent, because the lack of traverses meant that the defenders' fire had little effect. Furthermore, there was no strongpoint to which the defenders could retire. But he went on to say that every hour St Elmo held out would be of the greatest help to the rest of the island, and urged that the fort should not be evacuated for as long as possible.

The Grand Master had great faith in Captain Miranda, and took note of what he said, for he realized that his advice was sound. He then asked him to go over to St Elmo as governor and take complete control, as if he were La Valette himself. Miranda replied: 'Heaven forbid I should take charge of such a hopeless task! Afterwards people might say that it was I who lost the fort. Nevertheless, my Lord,' he went on, 'I wish you to have proof that I desire to serve the Order – for in doing so, I will serve my God and my King. Let me go to St Elmo as a simple soldier to join those valiant men. I will work in their company for the good of us all, and die with them.' La Valette, seeing that Miranda would not accept the command, allowed him to go, stressing at the same time how important the defence of the fort was. So Miranda returned to St Elmo, and the Grand Master gave orders that he should be implicitly obeyed.* As soon as he arrived in the fort Miranda had the alarm sounded,

* Although Miranda was not officially put in command, La Valette let it be known that Miranda had his complete confidence.

in order to test the discipline and to see what state the reserves were in. He gave such orders as he thought necessary for the defence, and sent a message to La Valette that, from a morale point of view, he should dispatch some money to pay the troops – for nothing makes soldiers happier than money. It was the Bishop of Malta, a very good Christian, who assisted the Order financially throughout the siege (as well as making many gifts to the poor and to the infirmary), who advanced the money for this. Miranda also asked for some barrels of wine. Then, when all was ready, he paid the troops. He had gaming tables set up, as well as bars, and the troops were naturally delighted.

La Valette was still very eager to recapture the ravelin. To find out if this were possible, he sent the marshal and Don Costantino Castriota to examine the situation with Miranda. They came back and said it would be a hopeless task, and would need more men than they had to spare. La Valette, therefore, gave up the idea and realized that the only hope of saving St Elmo lay in its defenders. Captain Fanton, on orders from the Grand Master, now went over to St Elmo by night to meet a spy. But while he was on shore waiting his boat's crew heard some noise, rowed off, and left the captain behind. He stayed there until daybreak and then, seeing no boat, rather than be taken by the Turks, he abandoned his arms and swam to safety.

After they had captured the ravelin and raised it to the level of St Elmo's walls, the Turks built a gun platform on it. Here they mounted two cannons and began a frontal bombardment of the fort. Dragut meanwhile carried on bombarding St Elmo from his side. The enemy also got into the ditch and began building a scaffold-bridge opposite the Post of Colonel Mas, but they were met by our gunfire and forced to abandon the project. They therefore began to take away stones from the wall, and to bring up scaling ladders in order to assault the post. Another bridge was built below the ravelin and fixed to the wall in front of it, but as soon as the defenders saw it, they determined to sally out by the ditch and see if they could burn it down. Nothing could be done from inside the battlements because of the great number of arquebusiers stationed on the ravelin [who would have shot them down when they showed their heads]. The sortie was made and there was a bitter struggle throughout the greater part of the night, but in the end our troops were forced to retire. All the same, they had managed to burn three of the supports of the bridge, leaving only two intact. All the knights and soldiers fought extremely well in this action, and inflicted many casualties on the Turks. We had a few wounded, and Sergeant de Medrano killed.

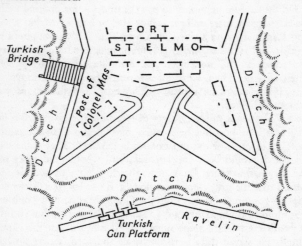

The Grand Master now learned that the Bailiff of Negropont was in a bad way from the arrow wound he had received during the battle for the ravelin. He also heard that Luigi Broglia, Governor of St Elmo, was ill. Broglia was a very old man and the strain and continual anxiety had so worn him down, that he told the Grand Master that, if it was his wish, he would retire. The Bailiff of Negropont sent a message to the effect that, although he was rather weak from his wound, he had no intention of leaving the fort. However, if the Grand Master wanted to send someone to take his place, he would willingly serve under him, but he was determined to stay in St Elmo as a simple knight, and to die for the Order.

Tuesday, 5 June. The enemy's fire was very heavy, Dragut's four-piece battery bombarding the tall tower which stands apart from the fort, the battery on the ravelin was bombarding the wall on its right. The Marsamuscetto guns fired on the apex of the Spur held by Colonel Mas, while the main battery fired on the whole of the curtain-wall as well as the tall tower. Inspired by Dragut, they were always trying to improve their fire, testing the defences at every point and probing for weaknesses. This day there was not a single safe place in all St Elmo.

La Valette, in view of the Bailiff of Negropont's condition, appointed Colonel Mas to act as his lieutenant. Hearing that the Turks had reconstructed the bridge yet again, he recalled Juan

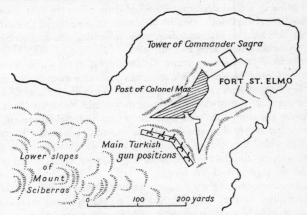

Vañon with one hundred of his soldiers from Mdina, and sent them over to St Elmo. Not for a moment did the bombardment slacken, and now the first two batteries on the heights above St Elmo were engaging St Angelo, as well as bombarding the boats, the windmills and the houses. At the same time, in order to get on with their bridge more quickly, as well as to protect their workmen, the Turks strengthened their garrison on the ravelin. Picked arquebusiers were stationed there to give covering fire to the men working on the bridge and those in the ditch.

Realizing that the Turks were not to be deflected from their objective, and that there was nothing they could do to stop them, the garrison of St Elmo decided to send Captain Medrano over to the Grand Master. He was to report on the situation, and to submit that it was the opinion of all that the fort could not be held. It had always had many defects, but now their defences were tottering, the enemy's bridge was almost ready, and the increased height of the ravelin meant that the Turkish fire now commanded the whole fort. The garrison could no longer defend themselves.

Captain Medrano went over to Birgu and told the Grand Master how the defenders of St Elmo felt. There is no need to explain what effect this news had upon La Valette. He knew perfectly well that the longer St Elmo held out, the greater hope there was for the whole island, since the delay gave them a chance to strengthen the weak points in the rest of the island's defences. He accordingly sent Medrano back to the fort to tell the defenders that the time was not ripe to come to a final decision. He asked them all to do their duty as they had always done, that he was more concerned for them than they believed and that according to the information he had received, relief could not be long in coming.*

Friday, 8 June. All, or nearly all, the knights in the garrison wrote to the Grand Master that it was certain death to remain in St Elmo. They begged him to give them permission to sally out and fight in the open. If fortune favoured them, they might manage to burn or destroy the bridge, or even drive the enemy from the ravelin. If, on the other hand, they should fail they would at least die happily. They added that, if they were unsuccessful, they would ensure that the water in the fort was poisoned, and the guns spiked. This letter bore the signature of fifty knights.

The resolution of these knights weighed heavily upon La Valette, especially since they had all acted together. Had it been a case of only one or two, he could have dealt suitably with them. As it was, he replied that he besought them all, and indeed ordered them, since they were all prepared for death (which would be certain if they were allowed to carry out their proposal), to stay at their posts in St Elmo. This was essential for the salvation of the Order, to which they were solemnly bound by their vows, and furthermore the relief force was hourly expected.

This day the Turks came at Fort St Elmo from every direction, some to reconnoitre and some to attack it. The latter launched a major assault which was both well-organized and determined. Their best and bravest men were detailed for the bridge. To begin with, they attacked with such wild courage that they were like *afion*-eaters -- afion is a kind of drug which has such violent effects that, after eating a little of it, men lose their reason and become quite without fear.†

Aware of the danger, our troops, under fire from the ravelin, repulsed them with the utmost valour. No less bravery was shown by the enemy as they charged forward. The bridge was the most critical place, for it was across this that the Turks hoped to reach our fortifications, where every means of defence – from cold steel to rocks

* This was the latest information that he had received in the dispatches from Don Garcia – brought by Salvago on the night of 3 June.
† Afion was almost certainly hashish.

THE ATTACK ON ST ELMO

a. Fort St Angelo: b. Birgu: c. Bormla: d. St Michael: e. St Elmo: f. Bighi Bay: g. Mount
Salvador: h. Corradino Heights: i. Gallows Point: k. Santa Caterina: l. Santa Margarita:
m. Marsamuscetto: n. Ships carrying relief to St Elmo: o. Dragut Point: p. Guns being
hauled towards St Elmo: q. Mustapha Pasha's pavilion: r. The loading of munitions in San

Giorgio Bay: s. The two Turkish commanders of the sea and land forces with Ochiali the Calabrian: t. Turkish troops carrying wood for the construction of gabions: v. A skirmish in which our troops were victorious: x. Two batteries bombarding St Elmo: y. Troops in camp during the bombardment of St Elmo: z. Turkish troops marching towards St Elmo: &. A skirmish in which several Turks were killed.

and fire – had been called into use. The attack lasted for seven hours, at the end of which the Turks retired with a loss of more than five hundred men, among them many Janissaries and fanatics. Our losses were forty dead, not counting the wounded. The knights, and all the soldiers of every nationality, conducted themselves most valiantly. After the Turks had withdrawn, a Spanish renegade shouted from their trenches: 'You have done well today, knights! But soon you will have to face what you seem to want so much – a general assault!'

The Grand Master immediately sent boats over to St Elmo to transfer the wounded to Birgu. Captain Juan de la Cerda was wounded by a musket-shot during this engagement, and his wound had only just been attended to after the Turks retired, when the alarm sounded again. He took off his bandage and, weak though he was, returned with great courage to his post. (His standard-bearer had been in Birgu since the day that the ravelin was lost, and the Grand Master kept him prisoner there until releasing him.)*

Every day La Valette was kept informed of the weakening position of St Elmo. The defenders could now hear the sound of tunnelling to the right of the first bridge, and they were afraid that the Turks were preparing a mine. Three knights, Don Francisco Ruyz de Medina, a Spaniard, Don Costantino Castriota, an Italian, and Antonio la Rochia, a Frenchman, were sent over by the Grand Master to see what chances remained of continuing to defend the fort. When they reached it, they found the garrison so confident that they would be withdrawn, that they had already destroyed half their ammunition and some of their arms. They had even begun to throw their cannon balls into the cistern, and were planning to blow up the fort. (It is rumoured that Colonel Mas was against all these measures.)

When the defenders learned the object of the knights' visit, they showed them the state of the defences, as far as was possible at night, and asked them for their opinion. Medina was doubtful whether the fort could be defended any longer, La Rochia was more hopeful, but Castriota said that there was no doubt that defence was still possible. All they needed to do was to erect inner defences behind the main curtain, and retire behind these. The defenders were astounded by his remarks and pointed out how small the fort was and that there were no materials of any kind for building defences. Moreover,

---

* See note on p. 56 concerning the cowardice of which Juan de la Cerda had been accused. Apparently his standard-bearer was held more culpable and for this reason had been detained in Birgu.

with the Turkish guns already commanding almost the whole of the fort and keeping up a constant fire on them, how could they possibly defend it? They would be glad to know any solution, and begged the three knights to stay until the morning – when they would be able to see the conditions properly, and so give the Grand Master an accurate account of their situation. As for them, they could see no possible means by which they could save the fort. 'But,' they went on, 'since you knights say that it *is* possible, stay with us and show us! Together we shall defend it to the death.'*

Don Costantino replied that he did not intend to stay, for they had not been sent across for that purpose. Colonel Mas then had the gate closed, and swore that they should not leave whether they wished to or not. The three knights then pleaded to be allowed to depart and promised they would make such a report to the council that the garrison would be withdrawn. If the Bailiff of Negropont had not used his wits, however, the three knights would have been forced to stay in Fort St Elmo. But, knowing that if this happened La Valette would be extremely annoyed, he had the alarm sounded with the result that every man dashed to his post. The whole garrison had been gathered in the square during the meeting, but now, by means of this trick, the Bailiff was able to let the three knights out of the fort.†

They reached Birgu at midnight and the council met immediately. The knights told the whole story, but denied that the rumour about the mine was true. They said that the Turks had only been taking away stones from the walls to make shelters for themselves. The council was divided over what action to take. Finally they decided to accept the opinion of the Grand Master and the admiral, both of whom held that St Elmo should not be abandoned, but reinforced. Don Costantino now proposed that he should undertake its defence, and La Valette told him to put forward his suggestions in council next morning.

In the morning, just as the council was about to debate the matter of St Elmo, two swimmers arrived from the fort, each bringing a letter. The first stated that the garrison was in a state of complete confusion and despair, and demanded that arrangements should be made for withdrawing them. In the second letter, it would seem that they complained about the Grand Master and the council for not

* It is not difficult to imagine the fury of the defenders, who had been fighting for days on end, when these well-fed 'staff officers' came and told them what to do.
† Presumably by means of a side gate on the Grand Harbour side.

having arranged the evacuation of the fort, and not sending them sufficient equipment for the defence. They asked for the things they needed to be sent over, together with reinforcements. But they stated that they were determined to hold the fort to the end. This second message was sent because they had been told that Don Costantino had offered to go and defend St Elmo, and if this had happened all the knights and soldiers would have felt disgraced.

Don Costantino stated that he would need five hundred men and also ammunition to go to the defence of St Elmo. But he added that he must be given complete authority over the knights that went with him. Although some still maintained that the fort ought to be abandoned, Don Costantino's offer was accepted. La Valette ordered him to make his preparations, to raise his standard and have the drums beaten to summon volunteers. The Grand Master gave permission for men to leave their posts and their companies, so that they might go to St Elmo. The money for paying these troops was again provided by the Bishop of Malta, and amounted to two thousand ducats. La Valette now wrote to the knights in St Elmo, saying he felt sorry that men who had already given ample proof of their bravery should abandon the fort. He reminded them also of the vows they had taken when they had entered the Order. He wrote to Miranda telling him not to forget the confidence La Valette had placed in him, and that, since he knew what Don Garcia had said [that the relief force would arrive soon], he must do his best to persuade the mutineers to stay and defend St Elmo.

When Miranda received the letter, he and the Bailiff addressed the garrison. So eloquent were they, that all with one accord said that they did not want to leave, but that reinforcements and ammunition should be sent over, and that they would all die in St Elmo. A message was dispatched to the Grand Master telling him of their resolve. La Valette at once sent one hundred soldiers under Orazio Martello, as well as money and ammunition. In order to make the enemy think that a much larger relief force was arriving, the troops carried with them a great number of banners.

Throughout this period, Commander Melchior de Monserrat, a knight from Valencia, had been visiting St Elmo on his own to keep an eye on things, and on a number of occasions he had told La Valette that the fort ought not to be abandoned. Being in need of an able man officially to replace Broglia as governor, La Valette asked Monserrat if he would be prepared to take over Broglia's duties. He at once replied that he was always willing and ready to do his

duty in the service of God and the Order. Accordingly he was sent
to St Elmo by the Grand Master and the council, and a devout
Capuchin friar of the Order of St Francis, to whom Monserrat was
deeply attached, accompanied him to the fort. On reaching St
Elmo, the friar preached a sermon, encouraging the garrison and
putting new heart into them for the fight. After hearing his words
the men felt strengthened and consoled, and ready for whatever
might befall. Luigi Broglia and the friar then left and returned to
Birgu.*

Among other events at this time, Commander Sagra was
wounded and was sent back to Birgu, his place being taken by
Antonio Gruño. We found out from a renegade who fled to Birgu
that, on the day that the ravelin was taken and the bridge was
attacked, the Turkish losses had been very heavy – much greater
than anything they had expected.

Fearing not only the loss of St Elmo but even greater misfortune,
La Valette now had a gun platform constructed on the site of the
windmills. Reinforced with earth and stones, it was built on a high
point from which it could give covering fire to the Post of Don
Francisco de Sanoguera, which was weak and vulnerable. When
the platform was finished, two large guns and two medium-sized
ones were mounted on it, covering the Marsa and the mouth of the
harbour. Hasdrubal de Medici was in command, assisted by some
Italian knights and soldiers. Casualties in St Elmo were heavy,
increasing every day. Indeed, in one day alone, the Turks killed
twenty-one of our sentries. Hearing this, the Grand Master sent a
dispatch to the Governor of Mdina ordering him to send down some
of the men who had sought safety in the old city.

Sunday, 10 June. La Valette had ammunition sent to St Elmo,
together with some new devices which are believed to have been
the invention of a knight called Ramon Fortuyn. These were barrel-
hoops covered with caulking material and saturated in a cauldron
of boiling pitch. Another layer of caulking material was then wound
round them, and they were once more dipped in pitch. This process
was repeated until they were as thick as a man's leg. During an
enemy attack they were set alight and flung among the enemy,
wreaking considerable havoc.

The Turks now began transporting loads of earth and fascines

---

* Technically, friars and clerics were not supposed to take part in fighting or bear
arms. As we shall see, however, in the attack on Senglea, there were some who were
as able with a sword as with a sermon.

into the ditch and, near the place where they had built their first bridge, they began raising ladders in order to attack the Post of Colonel Mas. But during the night our troops sallied out and, to the chagrin of the Turks, managed to burn down a large section of the bridge. In this action all the knights and troops taking part did very well. During the day the Turks bombarded St Elmo from all quarters right up to noon, when they made a large-scale attack – although it could not be called a general assault. A bloody battle followed, the Turks finally retiring with considerable losses, while we for our part had a number killed and a great many wounded. Once the Turks had withdrawn, the bombardment recommenced. They kept this up until the third watch of the night when they again attacked. There was no question of this being a reconnaissance, for they brought up a great number of scaling ladders and massed near the bridge and the Spur of Colonel Mas, shouting war cries and making a fearsome noise.

Although it was night, the immense number of flares and incendiaries used by both sides meant that there was no darkness. We, who were in the garrison of St Michael, could see Fort St Elmo quite clearly, while the gunners in St Angelo and the other positions were able to lay their guns by the light of the enemy's fires. The attack kept up until dawn. When the Turks retired they had lost over a thousand men, the highest percentage of their casualties being caused by our fire-hoops. We had sixty men killed and many wounded, the latter being sent over immediately to Birgu. The knights and soldiers of the various nations had fought with the greatest bravery, and not only they, but even the convicts and the mercenary oarsmen.

The firework-hoops were the most successful form of weapon used by the defenders in the great siege. Balbi, as here, attributes their invention to the knight Ramon Fortuyn, but the historian Vertot in his Histoire des Chevaliers Hospitaliers de Saint Jean de Jerusalem *(Paris 1726) claimed that La Valette himself was their inventor. Vertot describes how, 'During an assault, when the hoops were on fire, they were taken up with tongs and thrown into the midst of the advancing battalions. Two or three soldiers would regularly get entangled with one of these blazing hoops . . .' The flowing robes worn by the Moslems, although cooler than the armour, leather jackets, and so on, worn by the Europeans, were totally unsuitable for this kind of warfare.*

Monday, 11 June. Soon after midday the enemy, smarting from their heavy losses, began a furious bombardment. All morning they had been busy recovering their dead, while we were burying ours and sending our wounded over to the infirmary, where there were already more than two hundred.

During the night the Grand Master sent one hundred and fifty men to St Elmo together with ammunition, and a great number of baskets, mattresses, and piles of unravelled rope-yarn. These were designed to be used in place of fascines for repairing the defences. Meanwhile, in Birgu also, no time was lost in improving the defences.

The importance of the resistance of Fort St Elmo was, above all, that it gave the defenders time to put Birgu and the peninsula of Senglea (Fort St

Michael) into a complete state of readiness. Although La Valette had known right through the winter that the attack was coming, and done all that he could to improve the defences of Malta, the fact remains that the island was at that time nothing like so efficient a fortress as Rhodes had been.

Tuesday, 12 June. The Turks made no attacks, but maintained a furious bombardment all day and all night on every quarter of the fort. Our garrison in St Elmo took what cover they could, but had not a moment's rest. At midday Curtogli, one of the Turkish leaders, was killed by a shot from one of St Angelo's guns. He was in the trenches in front of St Elmo, observing the effects of the Turkish fire.

During the day Bajada arrived from Mdina with the news that the cavalry had captured a Janissary and two workmen. These had said that the Turkish losses on the previous night had been very heavy, and that all their wounded were dying. They said also that provisions were very scarce in the army, that the labourers were rationed to ten ounces of biscuit a day, and that many were dying from disease. Bajada was a Maltese who had once been a Turkish slave and spoke their language very fluently; he was a magnificent swimmer and served the Order very well throughout the siege.

A vessel was dispatched by the pashas to Tripoli, together with a barge and four galleys. These, so we learned from renegades, were full of sick and wounded. It was planned that they should return with provisions for the army, since they were short of honey, oil, raisins, butter, and other delicacies which the Moslems relish. Just about sundown Dragut sailed out of Marsa Xlokk with sixty ships. He followed the coastline until he was abreast Gallows Point,* whence he set course for Sicily. As we learned afterwards from renegades, he wanted his movements to be seen from Birgu, hoping to deceive the Grand Master and make him think that he was on his way to intercept some force destined for our relief. In fact, soon after nightfall, he returned to his former anchorage.

Wednesday, 13 June. A renegade came over to us with the information that there was considerable ill-feeling between the pashas and the Janissaries. The pashas were reproaching the Janissaries for calling themselves 'The Sons of the Sultan' and for their many other brave boasts, yet still they had not got the spirit to take a small, weak, and ruined fort, against which a bridge had already been laid. The

* Gallows Point was the southernmost point of the entrance to Grand Harbour, where Fort Ricasoli now stands. It was so-called because the gallows, where condemned criminals were hanged, were erected on it.

Janissaries, for their part, replied that when the artillery had levelled the walls, as it ought to do, they would show that they merited their reputation.

By day and night the enemy kept up a ceaseless bombardment of Fort St Elmo. At every hour there were calls-to-arms, while the Turkish reconnaissance forays were more like assaults, and on every occasion both sides suffered a number of losses. Their intention in all this was to wear down the defenders and give them no rest.

Thursday, 14 June. The bombardment continued ceaselessly throughout the day and night. After dark the Turks carried a lot of earth and bundles of brushwood into the ditch, but most of the wood was set on fire by the defenders. What was more, our artillery killed the Aga of the Janissaries when he was in their trenches.

Friday, 15 June. A major assault which lasted four hours was made in the morning. The enemy retired with heavy losses, but nevertheless attacked again in the afternoon and kept up the attack until dark. Neither of these attacks was what one might call a general assault, but they were made in force with great determination, and caused considerable losses on both sides. Over four hundred Turks and sixty Christians were killed, and we had as many wounded. These as usual were transferred to Birgu.

The commanders in St Elmo sent a dispatch to La Valette telling him the position, and saying that they expected a general assault next day. They asked for reinforcements of men, ammunition and other supplies. The Grand Master quickly met their demands. Throughout the dark hours the bombardment of the fort continued, the enemy making innumerable false alarms to harass our troops and prevent them resting. These alarms and excursions gave the defenders no time to repair the fortifications, since they were continually forced to stand to arms. All this was a clear indication that an assault was coming.

Among the many trials of the defenders was the necessity of having to procure earth for repairing the fortifications, the incessant bombardment having blown away all that had been taken into St Elmo before the siege started. Sappers were forced to go out and dig for it, and in the course of this many of them were killed.

VI

A GENERAL ASSAULT IS BEATEN OFF
AND DRAGUT IS KILLED

Saturday, 16 June. The general assault began at dawn. So great was the noise, the shouting, the beating of drums, and the clamour of innumerable Turkish musical instruments, that it seemed like the end of the world. Throughout the night preceding the assault the Turks had been assembled on the high ground near the fort, shouting at the top of their voices, as is their custom when praying. Two hours before dawn their priests absolved them of their sins, exhorting them to fight well and to die for their false faith. We knew this because we could hear first one man singing for a time, then all the army responding in unison. They kept this up until the sun rose, which was the signal for their attack. The men of St Elmo were ready to meet them.

At the appointed hour the general assault began. It was concentrated, determined, and ferocious, but was met with an equal courage and determination by the defenders. In fact, the courage and tenacity of the garrison was greater than that of the enemy.

The attack was marked by considerable use of incendiaries and fireworks on both sides. Our men suffered more from their own fire than they did from that of the Turks, due to the fresh westerly breeze which drove the smoke from their own fire, as well as from that of the Turks, into the defenders' eyes. But a far greater misfortune than this was that all the fireworks in St Elmo caught alight, depriving the defenders of these invaluable weapons, and also burning many of them to death.

At the peak of the battle, over thirty Turks, using scaling ladders, got on to the point of the Spur of the cavalier facing Marsamuscetto – the post of Colonel Mas. When the Grand Master saw from St Angelo what had happened, he had our gunners open fire on it to try and help the defence. But in the confusion and haste, so much a part of battle, the gunner laid his cannon further to the right than he should have done, with the result that the shot killed eight of the defenders. This accident could well have lost us St Elmo, if the knights and soldiers at that post had not displayed great calmness.

They did not withdraw from the position, but signalled St Angelo. The fall of shot had, in fact, been observed and the gunner corrected his aim. His next shot fell in the middle of the Turks on the fortification, killing over twenty of them. Our men killed the remainder with fire and cold steel, throwing their bodies down from the wall, so that not one of them escaped. From St Michael we could see one of our soldiers fighting like one inspired, with a trump in his hands.* We learned later that all the Turks who were on the Spur during this engagement were men of importance, sanjak-beys, galley captains, and chieftains.

The attack lasted for seven hours, and in each onslaught the Turks sent in a wave of fresh men. By the Grace of God they then retired, having lost over a thousand of their best and most distinguished warriors. The knights Hernando de Heredia and Don Juan Mascon assured me that, if the Turks had attacked once more, St Elmo would surely have been lost that day. There was not a man in the garrison who could stand to his post through fatigue. Our losses were one hundred and fifty dead, and a great many more wounded. Among the dead was Captain Medrano, who had bravely repulsed a Turk in the act of raising a flag upon the gabion. Medrano dashed forward to remove this flag but, before he could do so, an arquebusier shot him in the head and killed him. He was a man of the greatest courage as he had proved in every action.

Another who was wounded was Captain Miranda, but he refused to retire to Birgu. He had himself seated in a chair near the guns, where he stayed to the end of the action. The other wounded knights were transferred to Birgu. In this great assault, as I was told by the knights, it was not only they and their soldiers who fought well, but the convicts and the mercenaries, and indeed the Maltese – every one of whom fought as if he were a man of noble birth.†

The wounded, as well as the bodies of some of the knights, were quickly taken over to Birgu. La Valette gave orders that Medrano was to be buried among the Knights of the Grand Cross. This was the greatest honour that he could pay him, and one which he well

* Literally 'a fire tube'. Trumps were hollow metal tubes filled with an inflammable liquid mixture, an ancestor of the modern flame-thrower.

† In our century of 'democratic' warfare this may sound a little strange, but it must be remembered that at this time it was the essence of the knightly Orders that they should display greater courage than any common soldier. A soldier, who fought for pay, might be entitled to flinch or even run, but a knight was supposed to justify his privileges by superhuman courage. *Noblesse oblige* was a phrase intended to have a meaning.

deserved. Three regimental colours were captured by our men in this action, two complete and one torn. One of these had been the personal standard of Mustapha Pasha, and another of Dragut.

During the night La Valette sent further reinforcements to St Elmo under the command of Giarnu. They consisted of one hundred and fifty soldiers and a great number of sappers. With them they took more than two hundred mattresses, as well as tents, rope, and sails, for the garrison had no material with which to improvise repairs. While this was happening the Turks destroyed their camp in the village of St John. We reckoned that they were getting ready to leave, because of their great losses and because this camp was in the middle of their lines of communication between the fleet and their headquarters. Their real object however was to concentrate their forces, for they had already lost over four thousand of their best and most outstanding men. This same night La Valette sent two small fast boats to Don Garcia; one was captured by the enemy, but its crew managed to swim ashore.

Sunday, 17 June. The Spur was bombarded on its southern side by six cannons from the main Turkish battery. Other than this there was no further action during the course of the day, the Turks being engaged in recovering their dead from the ditch and burying them. All the same, the condition of the fort was desperate, and indeed almost hopeless. But twelve Italian knights, with the admiral's permission,* went to the Grand Master and volunteered to join the garrison. Accepting the fact that, as they said, they wished to fulfil their vows to God and the Order, La Valette praised them for their courage and thanked them. He told them that there would be plenty of time in which they could show their spirit, but he did not allow them to go. The fact was that Miranda had already sent him a message that the whole garrison of St Elmo was certainly doomed – as was proved on the following day.

Monday, 18 June. The bombardment of St Elmo continued, two further cannon having been added to the battery firing on the Spur. Ceaselessly by day and night, these eight guns kept up their fire. But, as if this was not enough, on the advice of Dragut, they erected a gun platform below the cave [near the water's edge, facing St Angelo]. From the counterscarp of the ditch facing towards St Angelo they

---

* The Admiral of the Order was almost invariably an Italian, which was the reason why the knights had to apply to him as the senior member of their Langue. La Valette had himself, at one time in his career, been Admiral of the Order, but this was a unique distinction.

now dug a trench extending down to the shore, near the place where the reliefs from Birgu landed. They had realized that as long as these relief forces could reach St Elmo there was no chance of capturing it, and this new trench would ensure that they could no longer get through. Like one who clearly understands the will of God, the Grand Master, as soon as he learned this, gave thanks to God that He

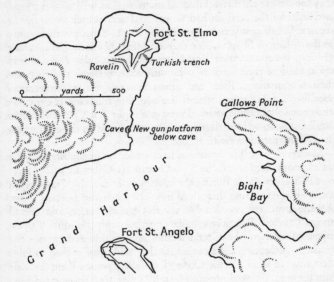

had allowed the Turks to be so slow in realizing their mistake. Had they done this at the very beginning, St Elmo would have been taken within four days. St Elmo lived, as they say, from day to day.

La Valette had never lost hope that the relief promised by Don Garcia would arrive, but, when it did, it was unfortunately at least ten days too late.*

One piece of news which comforted the Grand Master at this time was brought by a Lombard renegade, who arrived in Birgu saying that Dragut was dead, something that we were all glad to hear. The Lombard said he had seen Dragut laid low, his brains

---

* The Little Relief Force, as it came to be called, arrived off Malta on 24 June, but did not land immediately. Balbi has an entry on 3 July that 'it was just before dawn on 2 July that [we heard] the relief had landed'. He is not consistent, however, for the entry for 30 June shows that the relief force had already landed.

spattered from his mouth, nostrils, and ears. There was no chance of saving his life, the renegade maintained, and if he lied, the Grand Master might have him hanged. La Valette was very pleased at this, and the news was confirmed that night by renegades who arrived at the post of Don Francisco de Sanoguera, and said that there was no hope of saving the great corsair.

Dragut was killed by an accident. So as not to be taken by surprise in night attacks, the Turks used to build double trenches, and he was standing on the central scarp of one of these, when he saw that the gunners were aiming their cannons too high. He ordered them to aim lower. Their aim was still too high, so he again ordered them to lower it. Standing as he was with his back to the guns to observe their fire, a shot from one of them (which was now aimed too low) hit the trench behind him. A piece of rock thrown up by the cannon ball struck him on the head, and if it had not been for his turban he would have been killed on the spot. The very same shot killed the Master General of the Turks, Soli Aga.

Day and night we worked on the fortifications of Birgu and St Michael.

Tuesday, 19 June. The eight-gun battery with which the Turks had been bombarding the Spur was now augmented by a further two guns. The position was soon so battered that it would have been easy to scale. It was fully expected that the enemy would attack again, but they did not intend to do so until they had completed the new trench and battery near the cave. Both were under fire from St Angelo, but with little result since they were protected from that side, and the guns on St Elmo could not be turned against them in view of the fire from the enemy trenches and the intense bombardment. All that the garrison could do was to repair the fortifications with blankets, mattresses, and sails wetted with sea water as a protection against the enemy's incendiaries.

The new Turkish battery was almost ready. Their trench had gone so far that our men, drawing water to throw on the breastworks, were now in great danger. So many of them were killed that there was little hope of getting any more water. During the night, either by chance or possibly by treachery, a small powder-mill in St Angelo caught fire. It blew up and killed eight men who were working or sleeping there. As soon as the Turks saw the flame, they shouted for joy, thinking that the damage was greater than it was. But La Valette sent half a dozen cannon shots in their direction, and that soon stopped their bestial noise.

Wednesday, 20 June. The new gun platform designed to stop reinforcements landing at St Elmo was completed and, on the following
night, the Turks got the guns in position. Throughout the day and
night the Turkish bombardment was relentless. All the while they
kept on dumping brushwood and earth into the ditch, for which
purpose they had cut down the few trees and the little shrubbery that
there were in the island.* The garrison sallied out to burn the wood,
but it was so well mixed with earth that they had little success. The
situation was becoming desperate. We could no longer send boats
over to St Elmo, and La Valette could therefore no longer maintain
communication with the beleaguered fortress.

Thursday, 21 June. The feast of Corpus Christi. All day the Turks
kept up their usual bombardment, as well as getting ready new siege
devices for the reduction of St Elmo. We, for our part, did not fail to
honour this great and noble day as best and devoutly as we could.
The Grand Master took part in the procession, and himself carried
one of the poles supporting the canopy, along with the Knights of
the Grand Cross. The Bishop of Malta bore the Monstrance. All the
knights, commanders, and soldiers, excepting those on guard duty,
took part in the procession, together with the women and children,
and begged Our Lord to deliver us. The procession took a different
route from the usual one, so as to be under cover and not to attract
the Turkish fire. The Grand Master, with a napkin laid over his
shoulder and carrying his baton, served thirteen of the poor with
food. The Knights of the Grand Cross brought food and served it
to as many of the poor as asked for it. (This is a remarkable custom
of the Order and a most commendable one.)

The Turks continued to scour the island, and during the course of
one of these expeditions, their troops ran into a party of over twenty
Maltese horsemen. When the knight Tomas Coronel, who was now
in command of the cavalry, heard of this he and Vincenzo Anastasi,
who had taken the place of Juan Vañon, led a mixed party of
cavalry and infantry out of Mdina. They rescued the Maltese troops
in a battle during which many Turks were killed.

The garrison of St Elmo, even though they were at their last gasp,
never stopped trying to find some way to destroy the Turkish bridge.
They had attempted on many occasions to destroy it with gunfire,

---

* Although in succeeding centuries a great many more trees have been planted in
Malta, there are still quite large parts of the island where a tree is such a rarity as to be
a landmark. I have been told on one occasion: 'Go on half a mile until you come to the
tree, and then turn left.'

but with no success. Now an Italian soldier, Pedro de Forli, volunteered to go down on a rope from the wall and set fire to the bridge with a trump. This he did, but without success because the bridge was too well covered with wet earth.

Since they knew that no more reliefs could get through to St Elmo, the Turks felt confident that their next assault would succeed. They had also constructed a trench on top of the cavalier from which their arquebusiers commanded the whole position. As soon as a man showed himself, he was shot down, and there was no way in which the garrison could dislodge them from this new position – as Miranda had already informed the Grand Master. It was known by now that La Valette had little hope of saving St Elmo, for he could send neither supplies nor reinforcements to the fort. All that he could do was to beg Our Lord to show mercy to our brothers out of His infinite compassion, and to beseech Him not to allow the enemies of His Holy Faith to triumph. But, knowing that there was little hope for St Elmo, and anticipating that the main defences of the island would soon come under attack, he pushed ahead with the work on the fortifications of Birgu and St Michael. Day and night without any rest the garrison worked on the defences.

Friday, 22 June. The enemy bombarded continuously throughout the night, as well as raising many false alarms. Everything indicated that there would be a large-scale attack in the morning, and this is exactly what happened. At dawn the enemy came forward in their third general assault, and so great was the noise, and so violent their attack that it was truly terrifying – it was by far the most bloody and effective one they had made. Under covering fire from their guns they attacked by way of the bridge. But on this day they did not confine themselves to one place, but laid their scaling ladders against the walls at every point on the fort's circumference. There was not a single place where there was not some fighting going on. Both sides showed immense courage and endurance with consequent heavy losses.

It was around the bridge that the battle raged most fiercely, and at the spur of Colonel Mas' bastion. At this point the Turks were trying to breach the wall, while our men were trying to protect the gabions to which the enemy had secured ropes to pull them down into the ditch. The Turks attacking at this point came under heavy fire from the guns of St Angelo. Over by the bridge their attack was resisted with cold steel, with fire, and with rocks. But the worst casualties of the day were caused by the arquebus fire from the ditch on the cavalier, whence their snipers picked off all our leaders. The guns and powder of those who had fallen were picked up by the defenders, re-loaded, and directed against the Turks attacking the Post of Colonel Mas. At long last, to the fury of the Turks, they were forced to retire. – The attack had lasted six hours, and they had lost about two thousand killed and twice that number wounded.* They had intended this to be their final assault, and had attacked with every hope of complete success.

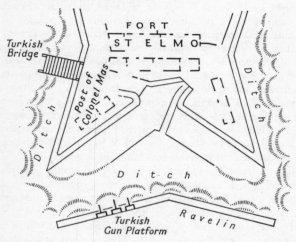

When the Turks withdrew there was not a single officer left in the garrison. Over and above this, five hundred Christians lay dead. There were only about one hundred men left, nearly all of them wounded, and without ammunition or any hope of relief. That night a swimmer was sent over from St Elmo to tell La Valette the position, and to beg him for assistance. The messenger said that there was not a man left in St Elmo who was not covered with his own blood as well as that of the enemy, and that they had no ammunition left at all.

God knows what the Grand Master felt but, so as not to dispirit the men around him in the square, he spoke as if with good heart. 'The garrison of St Elmo have taught the Turks a lesson. I trust in

* Balbi's figures must often err on the side of optimism. Many of them, no doubt, he got from Turkish deserters, who would surely have been eager to ingratiate themselves with the defenders by exaggerating the losses.

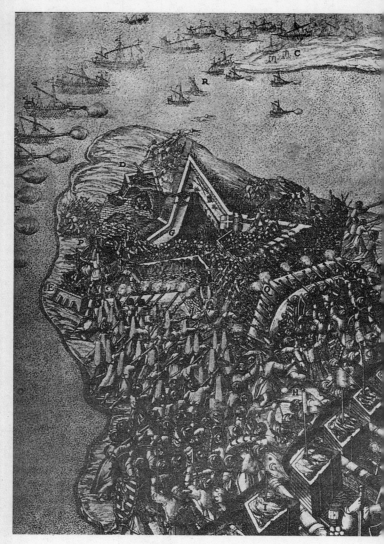

THE CAPTURE OF ST ELMO

a. Fort St Angelo: b. Mount Salvador: c. Gallows Point: d. Fort St Michael: e. The ravelin:
f. The Turkish fleet bombarding St Elmo: g. Fort St Elmo: h. Dragut killed: i. A gun
battery: k. A second battery: l. Mustapha Pasha: m. Piali Pasha: n. Ochiali the Calabrian:

o. Marsamuscetto: p. The Turkish breach: q. The Turkish entrenchment before St Elmo:
r. Armed frigates off St Elmo: s. An attempted escape by swimming: t. Guns firing on the
ships trying to bring relief: v. The galleon captured from the Turks: x. Galleys attempting
to bring relief to St Elmo: y. The headless bodies of knights thrown into the sea.

God that they will never take the fort.' Such were his words, but no man can tell what his feelings really were.

Despite everything, La Valette made an attempt to send reliefs to St Elmo. He sent over Captain Fanton in a galley without its mast. Knight Rostan de Laudun, Captain Villavecchia, and Romegas also went over in their own boats, but they were unable to get through. Not only did they come under fire from the trench on the shore, but they also ran into over eighty galleys just off Rinella Point. Mustapha was determined to take St Elmo on the following day.

That same night our poor brothers in St Elmo, realizing that no relief could reach them, made themselves ready to die in the service of Jesus Christ. They consoled one another in their great anguish and, although half-dead from exhaustion, they took no rest but worked all night on the defences. Unfortunately they had no water with which to drench the breastworks and, to add to their trials, the Turks kept up their bombardment all night, sounded alarms and made sporadic attacks. They did this so that, when morning came, the defenders would be worn out. The garrison of St Elmo, like men who know that the next day will be their last on earth, confessed one another. They besought Our Lord out of His infinite mercy to take pity on their souls for the sake of His Precious Blood which had redeemed them.

VII

ST ELMO IS STORMED BUT THE FIRST
RELIEF FORCE IS LANDED

Saturday, 23 June. At sunrise on this day, the Eve of the Feast of St John the Baptist – the Saint and Protector of the Order – the Turks made their final assault. To have resisted so furious an attack St Elmo would have needed not only a much larger garrison, but much better defences. Yet, few though they were, and despite the lack of ammunition, the garrison continued to stand firm for all of four hours. At the end of this time the enemy would still not have entered the fort if Medrano had not had the drums beaten and called the pasha to a parley. He explained to Mustapha how few men remained in the garrison.* The Janissaries swept into the fort first, by way of the high tower. They at once began hurling down stones on our men who were defending the bridge, calling out to their other troops to follow them into the fort since there were no more defenders left. Hearing this, the rest of their troops poured in, first by the Spur and then by the bridge.

There were, indeed, hardly any defenders left. All of them were wounded and, surrounded on every side, had no hope of resisting. They retreated into the church in the hope that some spark of humanity would permit the enemy to spare their lives. But as soon as they saw that the Turks were pitilessly butchering those who had surrendered, they rushed out into the centre and sold their lives dearly.

Only a very few Maltese saved themselves by swimming over to Birgu. Nine wounded knights were also saved, as they had taken shelter in the guard-house at the head of the ditch behind the church, and were able to surrender to the corsairs. Had they handed themselves over to the Janissaries, they would have perished to a man, but the corsairs managed to conceal them. Although Mustapha demanded that they be handed over, the corsairs refused to comply, but kept them so as to get ransom money.

* Medrano's hope that the garrison might be accorded the honours of war was disappointed. Mustapha Pasha, as we see, had no intention of showing mercy or taking any prisoners.

God alone knows how much the loss of St Elmo weighed upon the Grand Master, and upon all of us. But it had been lost with honour and at immense cost to the enemy. The Turks had spent over thirty days attempting to reduce the fort. It had cost them eighteen thousand rounds of cannon and basilisk shot, as well as the loss of some six thousand men. Among these were many of their leaders, not least Dragut. As I have said, they captured the fort, but at so high a price that they had little reason to rejoice.*

No sooner had the Turks stormed St Elmo than they tore down the banner of St John and hoisted in its place the standard of the sultan. They then spent the rest of the day planting flags and pennants on the walls – as is their usual custom. With the fall of St Elmo, their fleet, which throughout the siege had been anchored near Gallows Point, sailed into Marsamuscetto, dressed overall with flags and to the accompaniment of much noise and shouting. Although the flagship in the van fired two rounds, they did not waste their powder in other salutes, and we reckoned that they were keeping it for better use. This was quite unlike the practice of Christian galleys, which waste a vast amount of ammunition in firing such salutes.

This same night, the Turks lit a myriad fires in the Marsa, but I do not know whether they usually honour the Feast of St John, or whether they did it to celebrate the capture of St Elmo. Whatever the reason, it weighed heavily on our spirits for it is not thus that the knights are wont to honour the day of their patron saint.

Our losses in St Elmo were fifteen hundred men of all nations. Eighty-nine knights died in the siege, and twenty-seven were wounded and transferred to Birgu. Seventeen serving brothers were also killed.

The French, Italians, and Spaniards bore the brunt of the casualties. The Langue of Germany was only represented by a comparatively small number since it took the Germans much longer to travel from their estates to come to the defence of the Order.

The Grand Master sent a dispatch to the Governor of Mdina, telling him that St Elmo had fallen. La Valette said how deeply he felt the loss of the fortress, but that he accepted this act of fate, having faith

* The Abbé de Vertot records the story that, when Mustapha Pasha looked across from ruined St Elmo at the great bulk of Fort St Angelo, he exclaimed: 'Allah! If so small a son has cost us so dear, what price shall we have to pay for so large a father?'

in God's mercy not to desert him. He felt bitter that those of his knights who were away with the Order's galleys had still brought no relief after thirty-seven days. They should, he felt, have been able to bring over a relief force in three trips. But, his dispatches having borne no fruit, all he could do was bow himself before the will of God. Time was pressing, and he told the governor to inform Don Garcia of the loss, and to order the knights who were in Sicily to come to the island's relief at once. If even the smallest relief force had got through, St Elmo would have been held. He added that, in defending the fort, he had lost his best men. If Don Garcia was not quick to send aid, the Grand Master was afraid that when he did so it would be too late. He ordered the Governor of Mdina to send down to him the captains of the villages of Birkirkara, Birlestu, and Zurrieq, together with their men, before the Turks had had time to surround Birgu.

As soon as he had received La Valette's letter, the governor did as he was told, choosing the knight Tomas Coronel as his messenger. The latter crossed over to Gozo in a small boat which some Maltese carried down from Mdina to the shores of the strait. When he reached Gozo he was provided by Juanito Torrellas with another small boat. This was a craft made of ox-hides, held together by ropes (since they had no nails), and in it Coronel made his voyage to Sicily. He gave Don Garcia the news that St Elmo had fallen and, as we learned later, Don Garcia dispatched Stefano de Mari in a galley to Spain with this information.

Mustapha Pasha now made the Aga Mazot, a galley captain, Commander of Fort St Elmo. It was on this day that four galleys bringing reinforcements were sighted from Mdina. La Valette had already had news of them, but they were so slow in making their way up to the island, that he doubted if they would arrive before the Turks had cut off Birgu and St Michael.

This force, which was known as the Little Relief, did not in fact reach the island for several days. What is surprising is not so much that the galley captains hung about trying to find a suitable place and moment to land, but that they were ever allowed to land at all. Even though the Turks had made the elementary mistake of failing to secure Gozo and the northern half of Malta before they attacked the knights' citadels, Admiral Piali ought to have been able to blockade the island effectively. With the immense fleet at his disposal, it should have been impossible for any of the Christian galleys ever to get through. It would seem, however, that Piali's concern throughout the whole of the siege was to preserve his ships in the safety of Marsamuscetto.

Sunday, 24 June. The Turks, now being in possession of St Elmo, began to withdraw their guns to the Marsa so as to have them ready for whatever target they decided to attack first. We soon knew that this was to be St Michael. The defences of this peninsula and of Birgu had been considerably improved during the siege of St Elmo. With the shortage of available brushwood, La Valette had even had all the gardens stripped, beginning with his own, where there were four black mulberry trees, two palms, and a number of orange trees. At the same time he had apportioned the wells and water systems, so that everyone knew where to draw his own ration.

During the day we saw a ship leaving Marsamuscetto. This, we learned later, was bound for Constantinople carrying on board the guns which had been captured in St Elmo – twenty-eight cannon and the large culverin [that had been on the tower]. All the same, these were not the total number of guns in the fort, for the Turks never discovered the ones which had been buried under the debris caused by their bombardment. These we found later after the enemy had withdrawn from the island. During the day we saw four heads on the points of lances displayed above the battery bombarding the Post of Don Francisco de Sanoguera. It is believed that these were the heads of the Bailiff of Negropont, Commander Monserrat, Captain Miranda, and Colonel Mas. The Turkish barbarians did something even worse. They secured to planks and pieces of wood the bodies of the Christian dead – some mutilated, some without heads, and others with their bellies ripped open – and threw them into the sea so that the current would wash them over to Birgu. Their intention was to terrify us with so revolting a sight and to cow us into submission. But if such was their idea they failed, for the sight of our dead friends roused in us a desire for vengeance. As if this cruel deed was not enough to satisfy Mustapha, he bought from the Corsairs some Christians who had surrendered, and had them beheaded in front of the army. Being accused of cruelty by Piali, Mustapha replied that the sultan had ordered him to take no grown man alive, and this was tantamount to an order of 'no quarter'. There was now not a man who did not know that his only chance of safety lay in fighting, and every one from the highest to the lowest fought with added fervour.

During the night a galleot set sail to the east. We learned later that it took the news of the fall of St Elmo, and of the campaign up to date, and that Mustapha held out little hope of capturing Malta.

Monday, 25 June. The corsair Ochali Fartas set sail for Tripoli with five galleys. He had been appointed viceroy in succession to Dragut, and had had explicit orders from the pashas to collect all the available ammunition in Tripoli – something which Dragut had refused to do.* He also took with him the body of Dragut for burial. This dog had not died until half an hour after St Elmo was captured. He got no consolation, however, from its fall, since he had been unconscious from the moment that he had been wounded.

The death of Dragut was the greatest single disaster that befell the Turks in the siege. Balbi notwithstanding, some of the historians of the siege (including the Abbé Vertot) maintained that Dragut was conscious until his death. Mustapha Pasha is said to have sent a messenger to the corsair's tent in the Marsa with the news of St Elmo's capture. 'He [Dragut] manifested his joy by several signs and, raising his eyes to heaven as if in thankfulness for its mercies, immediately expired, a captain of rare valour and much more humane than these corsairs normally are.' During his attack on Gozo in 1544, when Dragut had lost his brother, he is said to have had a premonition of his fate. 'I have felt,' he said, 'in this island, the shadow of the wing of death! One of these days it is written that I, too, shall die in the territory of the knights.' The tomb of Dragut, greatest perhaps of all the Moslem corsairs, is still to be seen in Tripoli.

Tuesday, 25 June. It was now clear that the enemy intended to attack St Michael before Birgu. They kept the cannon which were bombarding the Post of Don Francisco de Sanoguera in place, while their engineers began to reconnoitre the heights of Corradino. They were clearly making preparations for establishing new gun platforms here, so as to bombard Fort St Michael and all the curtain-wall from Bormla to the Post of Don Francisco de Sanoguera. The Grand Master made an immediate inspection of this area and no time was lost in strengthening it wherever he indicated.

Wednesday, 27 June. The guns which had been bombarding the windmills and the boats now concentrated on the Post of Don Francisco de Sanoguera. As it was weak and ill-constructed, it soon began to feel the effects of the enemy's fire. But there was one advantage to this post; it could only be attacked by sea. We felt sure that

---

* Dragut, as Governor of Tripoli, had been responsible for its security, and had naturally been unwilling to reduce his own stocks.

the Turks would make two simultaneous assaults, one by land
[against the landward wall of the peninsula] and the other by sea
[against the Post of Don Francisco]. During this night we, who
were defending this post, sallied forth under Jaime de Sanoguera,
the nephew and first lieutenant of our commander. We cleared away
the rubble that had fallen from the walls as a result of the Turkish

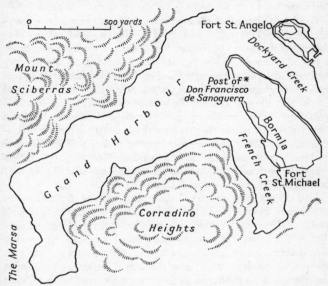

bombardment, and threw it all into the sea. Meanwhile Don Francisco had had some caissons made and filled with earth by hired
Maltese labourers and the mercenary oarsmen of his galley. He also
had a fighting platform built, as there was not already one in the
post.* Vincenzo Cigala, the Greek clerk of the galley *St Gabriel*, was
a tower of strength among the men who were drawing water to damp
the earthworks. He continually exposed himself to great danger, for
the Turks kept up a steady fire all night long, to try and hinder our
work.

During the night a boat was sent by the Grand Master to Don
Garcia, under the command of a Maltese, Antonio Xilla.

* A fighting platform was usually a high level mound within the defences, to which
the defenders could retire if need be, and from which they could fire over the walls at
the attackers.

Thursday, 28 June. A large Turkish force moved up from the Marsa and made some attacks in the direction of Santaren and the Bormla, where the houses are very close to the Posts of Aragon and St Michael. Our artillery opened fire and caused considerable casualties among the enemy. This engagement lasted for three hours and we lost two dead, but no wounded. La Valette saw quite clearly that these houses constituted a grave danger to the two posts.

During this period of the siege our cavalry was very active, harrying the Turks by night and by day. Knights and soldiers distinguished themselves on a number of occasions, the following being a typical example. When the armada descended on Malta, sixty Maltese men and women of varying rank had fled from their village and taken refuge in a cave near the sea, where they had been living for the past month. Among the women there was a very beautiful young girl, and when the refugees were discovered by the Turks as they overran the island, they reported the discovery of these people to a sanjak-bey. They did not, incidentally, in any way molest these Maltese, but the sanjak-bey, as we learned, went to their cave, bought the young woman,* and took her away while the other Turks were holding the Maltese in conversation.

Our cavalry captains learned about this, and one day rode down to the cave from Mdina. The Turks sallied out and a fight took place, in the course of which our men killed thirty out of the sixty Turks. The remainder, together with the sanjak-bey, seeing that they were defeated, took to their heels carrying off the young woman with them. Our cavalry charged after them, and the sanjak-bey, seeing that there was no chance of escape, cut off the maiden's head with one blow of his sword. Our men attacked him, and he was finally shot dead by an arquebusier. The rest of the Maltese were rescued and taken back to Mdina. I was told this story by Miguel Cali, a Greek who lived in Mdina and who took part in the rescue.

Friday, 29 June. Having noted during the previous day's engagement how great a danger the houses of Bormla were to the defence, the Grand Master now sent out some cavalry on reconnaissance, while he had a number of arquebusiers occupy the outermost houses. These they proceeded to fortify. Meantime he dispatched another strong force through the gate of Provence. These various actions were swiftly and silently carried out, and as soon as he was ready, he had one thousand Maltese sent out at the double, equipped with picks and bars of iron. They at once began to demolish the houses

* From her parents, presumably.

standing nearest to the Post of Aragon. Seeing what we were up to, the Turks on Corradino dashed down towards St Michael and Santaren, without waiting for any orders. They met with a fierce resistance, for our men had not only occupied the houses [of Bormla] but had also established themselves behind the walls, from which they opened fire on the Turks, killing many of them without exposing themselves to danger. The battle went on for three hours, our men, their powder exhausted, then withdrawing into the houses for a rest. The men who had been posted in the houses gave them covering fire, as did our gunners who manned all the cannon during this action and inflicted heavy casualties on the Turks.

The Maltese who were engaged in knocking down houses made good use of their time. A great many were totally demolished, and all the wood in them was taken into Birgu. As soon as La Valette saw that the whole Turkish force was coming into action he gave orders for our troops to retire, reckoning that enough had been achieved. We lost only one knight, but the Turks must have had many dead as far as we could judge. It was during this afternoon that we noticed a Turkish cavalryman at the head of a small band of men, riding from the Marsa towards Santaren. As soon as he came within range of our gunfire he brought out a white flag, as a signal that he desired to parley. Hearing of this, La Valette sent some men from the Post of Provence to Bormla, where they met an old Spanish slave, who said that he had been sent by the pashas to speak with the Grand Master. La Valette gave orders for him to be admitted, but first he was to be blindfolded as is customary on such occasions.

The man was brought before the Grand Master, and La Valette asked him why he had been sent. The slave replied that the pashas had sent him to ask La Valette if he would give an audience to their special envoy. 'If you know what the envoy has to say,' said the Grand Master, 'it is your duty as a Christian to tell me.' The slave, after much prompting, answered: 'The envoy comes from Mustapha Pasha and Piali Pasha to demand the surrender of the island to the sultan. He suggests that you do not display the same obstinacy as at St Elmo, or he will be forced to mete out the same treatment to you. While there is still time accept his clemency. All they want is this barren island. They will grant you, and all your people, your property and your artillery, a free passage to Sicily.'

Having heard him out, the Grand Master ordered: 'Take him out and hang him!'

The slave begged to be spared for the love of God, saying that he

o

was only a slave and that he had been forced to come with this message. Now the Grand Master had only given this order to frighten him, for he knew that the man was not to blame. But, acting as if he were only doing so at the request of some of the knights, he thereupon pardoned him. He told him to go back to his masters, but not to return on a similar errand. 'For,' he said, 'let this be known among the Turkish army: if any other man comes here with such proposals, I will hang him without mercy!' La Valette then told the slave to inform the pashas that he would not give an audience to their envoy, nor would he receive or speak to any of their messengers. Barbarians had no right to be received in audience. 'Do your worst,' he said, 'I do not care! My trust is reposed in Our Lord Jesus Christ, He will deliver us from your hands. More than that, He will give us victory over you!'

The slave was again blindfolded, led out by the Gate of Provence and taken between the two bastions of Provence and Auvergne. At that point, they unbandaged his eyes and let him see the depth of the ditch, and the height of the walls. They asked him what his reactions were and dumbfounded, he answered, 'The Turks will never take Birgu.' They blindfolded him again and led him out to the houses of Bormla, where he was released and sent back to the envoy. God only knows what a state of fear he was in, after what he had undergone.

When he reached Santaren where the Turkish envoy was waiting, we saw the party go in the direction of the Marsa, to make their report to Mustapha who had his headquarters there. During the evening the bulk of the enemy troops moved from the Marsa to the houses of Bormla [from which our men had now withdrawn], and to the heights of the Hermitage of Santa Margarita, where they pitched camp. But before this happened, we sallied out from St Michael and Birgu to hinder them, and a brisk action took place.

The Turks, having established themselves in the houses, now began to build a stone breastwork in front of St Michael, which extended from one side of the water to the other. They did the same from the houses of Bormla to Santa Margarita, and from there in the direction of the Posts of Aragon, Provence, and Auvergne. They made so great a noise in building these trenches and fortifications that it sounded as if all hell had broken loose.

Saturday, 30 June. The Turks now began to build four gun platforms, one of them on Corradino heights. It was clear that from this position, a very large one, they intended to bombard the peninsula of

St Michael from the extreme tip to the Grand Master's garden. A
second, designed to bombard us from the front, was sited at the
Mandra, while a third was near the vineyard of Pablo Miche, and
the fourth on Margarita hill. This was clearly designed to bombard
the bastion of Provence.

Our gunners did well today inflicting considerable damage on the
enemy, and killing a good number of the labourers carrying earth
and brushwood for the platforms. We noticed that those trees in the
Grand Master's garden at the Marsa which had been left standing,
were now cut down by the Turks for building the new gun platforms. During the morning a Turkish soldier came down near the
shore by the promontory of St Elmo. He called across to the Post of
Don Francisco de Sanoguera, where I was. Don Francisco told us
to ask him what he wanted, and the Turk called back: 'Send a boat!
I want to join you!' As soon as he heard this, Don Francisco gave
orders that none of us should show ourselves above the ramparts
since this might lead to the enemy catching sight of the man. His
nephew and lieutenant, Don Jaime de Sanoguera, was dispatched
to tell the Grand Master what was happening and La Valette ordered us to send a boat to bring the Turk across. It was to have a
trained boat's crew aboard who were to be on their guard against

treachery. Now as it happened, there was no boat ready outside the chain defence that day, and it would have taken some time to launch one, as well as drawing attention to it. So, when Don Jaime came back, his uncle ordered us to shout to the Turk that he must swim, for we had no boat. If he could not swim, we would go and help him.

The Turk, wanting to come over without any further delay, took off all his clothes and his armour. He kept only his shirt, which he wrapped round his head, and jumped into the water. At once three of our best swimmers, sailors from the galley *St Gabriel,* went out to help him. They came up with the Turk when he was not quite half-way across, and already so tired out that he could swim no further. However, with their help, he finally managed to make it.

The Turks meanwhile had seen what was happening, and were dashing down to the shore to stop his escape. But Don Francisco had expected this, and had got ready two light guns and a number of arquebuses. We were all up on the ramparts to give covering fire to the swimmers, and to the fury of the Turks we kept it up till the party were safely landed. Word was now sent to La Valette that the mission was accomplished, and no one was hurt, although the Turk was so exhausted that he could hardly breathe. Don Francisco now gave orders that he was to speak to no one until he had been brought before the Grand Master. Don Jaime and I then carried him to the captain's quarters, where the Grand Master's lions used to be kept. Here we offered him some refreshment, but he would take nothing except a drink of water because, he explained, it was Saturday and his fast-day. I then gave him a pair of trousers, and we took him to the Grand Master. The latter was very cordial and asked him publicly why he had come to join us. To this the Turk replied: 'I wish to be a Christian, as were my ancestors.' La Valette replied: 'You are welcome indeed!'

Later, after the siege was over the Grand Master rewarded this Turk and had him sent to Rome, where he was baptized by the pope and called Philip de Lascaris, the name of one of the great families of Greece. After this he went to Spain where the king, having heard from La Valette what good services he had rendered during the siege, gave him a pension for life and an appointment in the kingdom of Naples, where I have heard that he now resides. He himself told me some of the very useful information which he gave to the Grand Master during the siege.

The Grand Master had been greatly disturbed because for some time he had had no news from Sicily or Mdina. Furthermore, ever since 24 June, he had observed a signal rising from Mdina, smoke by day and fire by night, which he could not understand. When he told the Turk about this, the latter replied that a Christian relief force had already disembarked and had reached Mdina, but that he was the only Turk to know about it. He said furthermore, that the first major assault would be very fierce, and would be made by land and sea simultaneously.

The Turkish deserter whose story Balbi recounts, was one of the most interesting minor figures in the great siege. Later historians, better informed on some points than Balbi, make it clear that he did not just receive the name Lascaris on his baptism by the pope. He was born a Greek of this ancient and noble family, which had numbered three Byzantine Emperors among its ancestors. Lascaris had been taken from his family when young, and had risen to high rank in the Turkish army. Familiar with all its techniques in warfare, he was also acquainted with the detailed plans drawn up by Mustapha and Piali for the siege of Malta. The reasons for his desertion are recorded by Vertot: 'The heroic courage which the knights showed in abundance every day, had excited his compassion; he reproached himself for fighting in company with barbarians, with men who had caused the death of most of the princes of his own family and forced the others — ever since the capture of Constantinople — to seek exile in far-off lands.'

Sunday, 1 July. All day the enemy were busy constructing their gun platforms. They shouted across to us from their trenches telling us what we were going to suffer as soon as these were completed. We, for our part, were engaged in strengthening the more important places that we expected the enemy to bombard. Praise be to God, they had wasted so much time on St Elmo, that we had been able to get our fortifications reinforced — although we were always lacking in such essentials as earth and bundles of brushwood.

Monday, 2 July. This was the day when we heard from Mdina that a relief party had landed. They numbered seven hundred men, among them forty knights of the Order and twenty gunners. Melchior de Robles, a knight of Santiago, and general of the garrison in Sicily, was in command, a brave and very experienced soldier. Just before we got the news, the Grand Master had conceived the idea of bringing a boat overland from Birgu to Marsa Scala, through the Gate of Castile. By this means he hoped to be able to send a dispatch to Sicily. He had thought of this, as the Turkish fleet was no longer based on Marsa Xlokk, but was on patrol at the mouth of Grand Harbour. As it turned out, we were not able to transport the boat.

Tuesday, 3 July. The Turkish gun platforms were now ready, and they immediately began to bombard us with twenty-five heavy guns. Six on the heights of Santa Margarita bombarded the bastion of Provence; a further six at the Mandra bombarded the wall of St

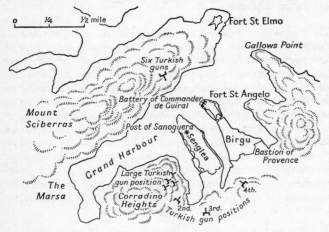

Michael from the front; four in Paolo Miche's vineyard bombarded the Post of Don Carlos Rufo; from Corradino, where they had three cannon and one enormous basilisk, they bombarded Bormla and the surrounding houses; finally, six guns sited on the promontory of St Elmo opened fire on the Post of Don Francisco de Sanoguera, St Angelo, and the battery of Commander de Guiral.

As I have said, it was on 24 June that the four galleys bringing the relief force had been sighted from Mdina, and since then they had been making daily signals. It was just before dawn on 2 July that Bajada arrived with the news that the relief had landed, and that they had been brought down by Don Juan de Cardona in two Sicilian galleys and two belonging to the Order. The Grand Master was in a quandary as to how so small a force could get into Birgu without considerable risk, since we were surrounded by so many enemy troops. He consulted Lascaris, who said that the best route for the relief to take was down the coast from Mdina as far as the inlet of Salvador and from there to be ferried over to the Post of Castile. He was confident that if they took this route they would not run into any Turks, and he offered to lead the way. Bajada agreed with him, saying that he had never seen any of the enemy in that direction. The council concurred with this plan, and Bajada, in company with some other good guides, was sent back to Melchior de Robles with instructions to take this route.

Having received the Grand Master's orders, Marshal de Robles had horses got ready for those who needed them. One hour before sunset on 3 July, he led out his party from the city and, taking no notice of those who had advised him against the plan, marched his men all night. They maintained strict order, silence, and discipline. Nevertheless Marshal de Robles was on tenterhooks for they passed within a stone's throw of the enemy lines, and it seemed impossible that they should not be discovered. Although they must have been heard, they were, thank heaven, never attacked, and they reached the rendezvous on the following morning, just two hours before dawn.

The boats were waiting for de Robles, and he saw his men embarked before he himself came over – the last man into Birgu. He was delighted with the behaviour of his troops, and La Valette and the rest of us were as pleased as he. This was the third lot of reinforcements which the King of Spain sent to help the Order.* We were in dire need of them, and if they had not got through we could never have withstood the first great land and sea assault, let alone the others that followed.

The landing of the relief and its safe conduct was due rather to the mercy of God than to human foresight. I remember one day, hearing Marshal Robles (who was standing at the Post of Don Francisco taking some refreshment with a few of the knights who had brought him to inspect the post) say that he and Don Juan Cardona had been ordered not to land with the relief force if St Elmo had fallen. On the day that they reached the island, however, an hour before dawn, as they put into Piedra Negra, they sighted a light in a cave. This had been set there to lead them in, so they beached the ships and lowered the gangways. The first man to land was a French knight called Quincy who, when he had been in Sicily, had come to the following arrangement with the knight Salvago. This was, that as soon as the galleys reached Malta, he would land first and see that, if St Elmo had fallen, the news was kept secret. Of course, when he did land, he quickly learned from some Maltese that the fortress was lost. He

* Prior to the siege, two separate detachments of Spanish troops – in one of which Balbi served – had been sent to assist the garrison.

gave them strict orders not to reveal this and told them, if they were asked, to say that it was still holding out. The troops heard this news, leapt ashore, and the galleys were soon back at sea.

On the day they landed it was God's will that there was a heavy mist,* and so our troops were able to reach Mdina without being seen by the bands of Turks foraging in the island. If they had been seen, they would have had a hard fight to get through, for it is all of six miles from Piedra Negra to the old city. When they did reach their destination, great was their dismay to learn that St Elmo had already fallen.

At this point a Greek, who had taken refuge in Mdina, was tempted by the devil to go and tell the enemy that the relief force had arrived, as well as how to prevent them getting down into Birgu. But it was God's will that one of our sentries on the walls saw him just as he slipped out, and the cavalry was sent to catch him. They brought him back into Mdina, where he confessed what he had been about to do. He paid for his treachery by being quartered.

Among the many French, Spanish, and Italian knights and private adventurers making up the Relief Force, there are two Englishmen recorded. Balbi gives their names as Ivan Smilt – John Smith? – and Eduardo Stamle – Edward Stanley? They were most probably English Roman Catholics who may have been resident in Rome along with many others who were self-exiled from Queen Elizabeth's Protestant England.

The Maltese, Bajada, who is mentioned by Balbi in this day's entry, as well as on several other occasions, has become an almost legendary figure in the island. Many are the stories told about him in Maltese folk-lore, where he has become something of a Mediterranean Robin Hood. There is a street named after him in the fishing village of St Paul's Bay, the scene of the final defeat of the Turks.

---

* Not unusual in Malta if a sirocco is blowing, but commoner in the autumn than in mid-summer.

THE BOMBARDMENT OF BIRGU AND
THE POST OF CASTILE

a. Fort St Angelo: b. Birgu and the Post of Castile: c. The windmills: d. Mount St Elmo:
e. Marsamuscetto: f. Dragut Point: g. Fort St Elmo: h. Mount Salvador: i. Boats transporting

tillery to Mount Salvador: k. Gallows Point: l. Mustapha Pasha: m. Artillery being
isembarked: n. Piali Pasha: o. Turkish janissaries: p. Mount Calcara: q. The Belvedere:
r. Sappers at work: s. A group of Turkish officers.

VIII

MUSTAPHA PLANS TO ATTACK ST MICHAEL FROM THE SEA AND DON FRANCISCO DE SANOGUERA IS KILLED

Wednesday, 4 July. The Turks learned today from some prisoners they had taken, that the relief force had reached Birgu. They had captured these men of ours while they were engaged in taking back the horses to Mdina. In their anger, the enemy bombarded us relentlessly all day, concentrating on the houses.

Thursday, 5 July. Having added a further twelve guns to their batteries, the Turks kept up a ceaseless bombardment by night and day. Again they concentrated on the houses, and killed many women and children who were in the streets, or working on the defences. When he saw this, La Valette refused to allow Christians to be exposed to such danger. He gave orders that slaves should do the work on exposed positions, and they were sent out chained together in pairs. The Grand Master hoped, that when the Turks saw who they were, they would hold their fire. But he was quite wrong, for the slaves were shot down by the score. During the whole siege over five hundred slaves were killed like this. These poor creatures grew so exhausted from their incessant labours that they could hardly stand from fatigue, and preferred to have their ears cut off, or even be killed, rather than work any more.

Seeing that the batteries had been reinforced, and that they were having a devastating effect, La Valette ordered the Commander of the Arsenal to have old ropes cut up and made into bundles with cords around them. These were designed to replace the brush wood which we lacked and, mixed with earth, they were used for repairing the fortifications. The sick and disabled slaves were kept busy the whole time making fuses for the arquebuses, while the Turkish renegades were solely employed making arquebus and other small-shot. Night and day our blacksmiths' forges were working on repairs to the guns as well as making nails, and doing every conceivable type of iron work.

Friday, 6 July. A general bombardment began at dawn. Since their fire was doing little damage to the posts of Provence and St Angelo, they concentrated twenty guns on St Michael. During the day we saw six boats in the Marsa, which had been brought overland from Marsamuscetto.

Mustapha had hit upon a master stroke in dragging these vessels over half a mile of rocky territory. Up to this moment the defenders had felt confident that the waters of Grand Harbour from St Angelo down to the Marsa were safe. They now found that as Lascaris had warned La Valette, the Turks were going to attack the Peninsula of St Michael by sea, as well as by land.

Saturday, 7 July. Aware that our reinforcements had got over by way of Salvador, the Turks now took possession of the hill. They erected a very large gun platform up there, as well as posting a strong guard to hem us in. There were now twelve vessels in the Marsa, all of which had been brought overland from Marsamuscetto, and we felt sure that we might expect an attack from the sea. To guard against this, we set a watch at the Post of Don Francisco on the foreshore, and also at Bormla. At the points where the great chain closed off the entrance [between St Michael and St Angelo] we always had six boats stationed on both sides to guard it.

Sunday, 8 July. Grand Master La Valette, alert as ever, saw that the new gun platform on Salvador was nearly finished, and gave orders for a number of houses that were threatened by it to be demolished. He himself moved his own quarters to the house of his majordomo, Scambila. At the same time he had all the streets in that area barricaded with stone walls, so that the gunners and arquebusiers on Salvador could not continue to inflict so many casualties – for they were at close range and could see their targets quite clearly. Some other houses between the Posts of Castile and Germany were demolished at the same time, while work began on a ditch behind the walls. Over two hundred paces long, it was strengthened with innumerable earth-filled gabions and had plenty of casemates cut into it.

Daily the number of boats in the Marsa increased, and on Saturday we had counted over thirty. Some were large and some small, and it was quite clear that we would soon have to undergo a major assault.

Monday, 9 July. The Posts of Castile and Germany came under fire from thirteen guns on Salvador. Fortunately the fire was mainly directed against the houses and did little damage, thanks to the foresight of the Grand Master.

While this bombardment was going on, the enemy attempted to capture the ditch of St Michael at the point where there were four great casks filled with earth standing on our side of the ditch, and there were many casualties in the fighting which took place. When our men wanted to sally out, they used a small opening in the wall at the Post of Marshal Robles and Don Carlo Rufo. Marshal Robles had taken command at this point after his arrival, although Don Carlo also stayed there until he was killed.

Tuesday, 10 July. A messenger reached us from Don Mezquita, Governor of Mdina, with the news that there were eighty galleys and sixty ships ready at Messina bringing the troops of Don Philip, King of Spain. This messenger had a hard job getting through and had to swim across from the promontory of St Elmo, to reach the post of Don Francisco de Sanoguera.

There were now over sixty boats at the Marsa of various sizes. Taking advantage of Lascaris' information that they would certainly make an attack by sea, La Valette took every precaution to bring the defences of St Michael to the ready, and whatever the Grand Master reckoned was best for the defence was immediately carried out. Beginning with the Post of Marshal Robles, right up to the end of the Peninsula (the Post of Don Francisco), he had a line of heavy piles driven into the sea bed. They were set twelve to fifteen paces apart, and about twelve paces off-shore. The piles were linked by iron bound cross-pieces, and a chain passed through a hole in each of the piles and connected them all together. The whole defence was so well constructed that it was strong enough to resist a galley rowed against it at full speed. This off-shore defence was built at the Grand Master's orders, not only to stop the Turkish boats landing, but to force the attackers to jump into the water before they could get ashore. The idea was that they would get completely drenched, which would be greatly to the disadvantage of the arquebusiers and archers in their long robes.*

The usual heavy bombardment went on. Round about noon one of their guns in a six-gun battery on Corradino exploded, probably because they had neither been cleaning it, nor allowing it to cool. In the explosion it set off all the ammunition stacked near by. Over forty Turks were killed, and among them there must certainly have

---

* The more obvious disadvantage, that Balbi does not point out, was that the powder, muskets, and bowstrings of the enemy were almost certain to be damaged by the water.

been some distinguished officers. The battery concerned fired no
more during the day. We saw the whole of this incident from our
posts on St Michael. Meanwhile the number of boats continued to
increase in the Marsa, a great many more arriving during the course
of this day.

Wednesday, 11 July. At dawn four Turks went down from Corradino and swam under water to the Post of Bormla. Each of them had
an axe in his belt and, as soon as they reached the chain, they got
astride it and tried to cut it through. They were seen by our sentries
and the alarm was given. We immediately opened fire, fearing that
if they were successful the great assault would take place during the
day. Quick though we were in spotting these men, we could not
get up on to our parapet, for they were being given covering fire
by their finest arquebusiers from the trenches on Corradino. Despite
the fact that they were over six hundred paces away, they never
missed.

In the midst of all this, four Maltese from the Post of Bormla*
(near the point where the chain was being attacked) leapt down
from the battlements with swords, bucklers, and helmets. Their
spirit and ferocity was such that – not just for Maltese, but for any
other nation – it would have been impossible to show greater
courage. They fell on the Turks with such violence that they were
forced to abandon their task, and take to the water. But although
the enemy's fire was hot, the Maltese swam after them, killed one
of the Turks, and wounded the others. In this way the Turkish
attempt was frustrated, and our men got back in a hail of musket fire
without suffering any casualties.

We had further reason to expect an attack this day, for fifty
galleys came round from Marsamuscetto and landed a large party
at Rinella. These, we learned, were labourers sent to work on the
gun platforms at Salvador. We came under a heavy bombardment
throughout the day and night from ten of their batteries. During the
night, I was in the Post of Marshal Robles, together with a number
of soldiers from other positions, since it was usual to send us wherever
we were needed. Marshal Robles, armed with sword and shield,
went out with over two hundred of us to the foreshore. Here we fell
upon the Turks who had captured the earth-filled casks by the ditch,
and put them to flight. There were over three hundred of them and
we killed more than thirty. Those who fled took shelter behind their

---

* The Post of Bormla was on the side of the peninsula that faced Corradino.

trenches on the far side of the ditch. We lost four men, two being Spaniards from the Marshal's company, and two Maltese.

Friday, 13 July. The incessant and general bombardment kept up all the time. It was mainly concentrated on the Posts of Don Francisco, Bormla, and St Michael. The fire was so heavy that we were sure a major assault was imminent. Another sign was the number of boats in the Marsa, now over eighty, some of them very large. All the time, our men kept up their work repairing the defences.

Every night the Turks used to make their prayers and devotions with such a shouting and screaming that it was really laughable. One of them would first of all sing for a long time on his own, and then the others would all reply with a monstrous caterwauling. Another thing they used to do was to shout across from their trenches at us, renegades in their ranks saying whatever came into their heads, and we replying in a similar vein. Among the renegades there was a corrupt Maltese, who could speak all our languages. He called over to Paulo Micho and Paulo Daula, two very fine old Maltese, and told them who he was. He went on to say that the pashas were well aware that the Maltese wanted to be free and not vassals, and that they wanted to avenge themselves on the knights, by whom they were so badly treated in every possible way. It was well known, he said, that there were very few knights and not many more mercenary soldiers. Why, then, did not the Maltese kill them and regain their former freedom? The pashas promised, in the name of the sultan, that they would treat the Maltese better, and look after them in every way – which was more than could be said of this wretched Order they now served.

These two fine old men answered him briefly: 'You are lower than a dog! We want no advice from a man so damned as you. We would rather be slaves of St John than companions of the sultan!' Seeing that his words had no effect, the renegade shouted to Paulo Micho that he would never enjoy his vineyard, he told him also to look after his money until the Turks came in – and that would not be long. He added that if he wanted to be saved, Paulo should tell him where he could be found. He would save him and five others since, on account of his valour, he had some influence with Mustapha. Good old Paulo Micho shouted back: 'I have been repaid for my vineyard in Turkish blood. I have trust in God that, even if you Turks destroy it, I will plant another and water it with the same blood – and that will make it a good deal richer! For my money,' Paulo added, 'I have enough trust in God to know that it will never be allowed to fall into the hands of a scoundrel like you. As for wishing to find me, whenever you think you are going to break in, look where the battle is fiercest. There you will find me, old as I am with my sword and my shield, defending my God, my country, my wife, and my children.'

That was the end of the conversation, but afterwards La Valette gave orders that we should not reply, or talk to renegades. The best way to treat them was with silence.

As the enemy's intentions were now quite clear, the Grand Master allowed no time to be wasted in repairing the damage caused by their bombardment. He also gave orders that those who were in charge of the incendiaries and fireworks should see that they had a good store of them ready, and finally that all the commanders should exercise the greatest alertness. A great many slaves working on the earthworks and defences continued to die under the enemy's fire. During the night La Valette had a floating bridge, which had been constructed of barrels and planks, towed into position between Birgu and St Michael, so that the latter could be quickly reinforced if the occasion arose. He had not had this done earlier so that the enemy would be taken by surprise, and would not have time to destroy it.

Next morning, as soon as the enemy saw the bridge, they opened fire on it and did some damage. But on the following night, to prevent this, it was towed over nearer to St Angelo. The result was that, although the batteries on St Elmo were able to bombard it and even hit it, it did not suffer any great damage. In St Michael we were glad enough, God knows, when we saw this bridge, for we took it as a clear sign that now we should be able to win.

Something which I must not forget to mention is that, before the arrival of the relief force under Marshal Robles, his Holiness the Pope, Pius IV, sent us a relief for our souls. This was a plenary indulgence and a pardon for all sins (something that the Church usually gives its children under such circumstances). There was not an adult man or woman who did not earn it with their great devotion, and with the secure hope that, if they fell in the siege, they would find a place in heaven.

Saturday, 14 July. While we were fully engaged in making good the damage, the bombardment never let up. We had been warned by the renegades that a general assault would take place next day. The places likely to be attacked were the Posts of Don Francisco, the Bormla, and the Post of Marshal Robles; these were the weakest points. There were now so many boats in the Marsa that they looked like another armada, thirty of them being large enough to hold eighty men apiece. We could not understand quite how it was, but they seemed to increase in size – so we guessed that they were being built up with protective superstructure against our arquebus fire.

During the uneasy night that followed, their priests kept up an endless chanting – just as they had done before their general assault on St Elmo. We knew then what to expect when morning came. Marshal Robles warned the Grand Master, who ordered the captains of the reserves and their men to stand by. At the same time he had plenty of ammunition and incendiaries brought up to the threatened positions.

Sunday, 15 July. An hour and a half before daybreak it was obvious that the Turks were about to launch their general assault. There was a great noise and bustle in their boats, now numbering over a hundred. From where we stood we could see great numbers of men embarking, as well as siege material and weapons being loaded aboard. At the same time as they were embarking their troops and getting ready, other men were being landed at Rinella and Gallows Point. These were intended to join forces with their comrades from the Marsa in the attack on St Michael. The distance between the two points was over three miles.

As soon as these assault parties were ready, a fire was lit on the platform at the Mandra, and at once another one answered it from the promontory of St Elmo. These were clearly the signals for the attack to begin. The sun was now up and we could see the boats more clearly. Their sides were built up with sacks of wool and cotton, and they were lined with magnificent-looking troops. They certainly made a fine sight – almost beautiful, if it had not been so dangerous. Three thousand of the flower of the Turkish army, as we learned later, were embarked in these boats. With them were the best troops belonging to Dragut and the Ruler of Algiers. Even the rank and file wore scarlet robes, and there were many in cloth of gold, and of silver, and of crimson damask. Armed with the fine muskets of Fez, scimitars of Alexandria and Damascus, and magnificent bows, they all wore splendid turbans.

As soon as they saw the signal fires – signals that would send them to hell – their boats got under way. As they drew nearer we saw that in the vanguard there were a number of men with long hair, wearing very large hats. They had books in their hands, from which they seemed to be reading prayers – but in fact, they were only consulting the omens, as is their custom.* These, they said, were good. When they had finished, their boats retired, while the rest of the troops came on to the attack at full speed along the whole shore line between Bormla and the Post of Don Francisco. They hoped to break through the chain, but when it held firm, the assault parties were forced, in order to get ashore, to wade through the water between the chain and the land. Even those who got least wet were up to their waists in water. Yet in spite of everything they came on to the attack with immense courage and determination, and with so many war cries, and such a crackle of arquebus fire, that it would undoubtedly have caused panic among men unaccustomed to war.

Captain Don Francisco was ready for them, as was his nephew and the men under his command (a little less than sixty of them). As soon as he had seen them embarking, Don Francisco had assigned each man to his post. Meanwhile Don Jaime was engaged in opening a covered embrasure that we had got ready for an attack like this. It was designed to give covering fire right up to the Post of the Sicilians, which was very low and flat. We had mounted two mortars at this point, one all ready to fire and the other one loaded. However, so swift was the Turkish onslaught that we did not have time to make use of them – some say it was the gunners' fault. This embrasure and the whole Post of Don Francisco were therefore only defended by our strong pikes, swords, shields, and stones. It was at this very point that the Turks made their first attack, just where the Spur was very low and levelled almost flat by their gunfire. At the point of the Spur, however, there remained two earthworks for our defence. Don Jaime de Sanoguera hastened there with sword and shield, fighting and putting heart into his men, who – on this day as on all others – bore themselves like good soldiers. Although Don Jaime's face had been burnt by gunpowder, he never left his post.

The Turks meanwhile had got up on to the traverse with their scaling ladders; being very low it was not difficult to climb. A sailor from the galley *St Gabriel*, a Provençal called Piron, defended the point most bravely until he was shot dead, when another man

* Balbi, naturally, has nothing but scorn for the Moslem faith. The imams, of course, were not 'consulting the omens', but reading appropriate passages from the Koran, such as the passage in VIII, 15: 'O you who believe, when you meet those who disbelieve marching to battle, do not turn your backs to them. Whoever turns his back on that day . . . incurs the wrath of Allah, his destination is hell and an evil end.'

called Piron, a Genoese from the same galley, took his place. He, too, fought like a lion, and I must not forget to mention that the knight Adorno was also in the fight at this point, as well as achieving miracles on the earthworks and down by the sea-shore. Adorno was among the very first who jumped down outside our defences.

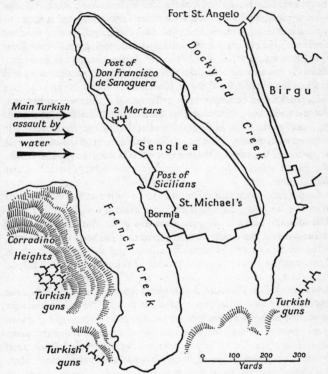

Fort St. Angelo

Post of
Don Francisco
de Sanoguera

2 Mortars

Main Turkish
assault by
water

S e n g l e a

D o c k y a r d   C r e e k

B i r g u

Post of
Sicilians

St. Michael's

Bormla

F r e n c h   C r e e k

Corradino
Heights

Turkish
guns

Turkish
guns

Turkish
guns

0   100   200   300
Yards

As if it was not enough that we were few in numbers, and our defences weak, we suffered a further disaster. Ciano, one of the soldiers at this post, was lighting an incendiary to throw among the enemy, when the fire spread among all the others. Ciano and a great many other troops were burnt in the ensuing blaze. Having lost our fireworks and incendiary bombs, we were now forced to rely on stones, but we had plenty of these and did even more harm with them than we would have done with the incendiaries.

H

The moment that Don Francisco had seen the boats making for his post, he jumped on the parapet armed with sword and shield. He was worried that they might take it by frontal assault, since it was so low and so badly damaged. Hard on his heels came Nicolo Rodio, his assistant clerk, and I, all of us firing our arquebuses at the enemy, who were already at the foot of the battery. But the Turks were so close, and we so few in number, that we found it better to lay aside our arquebuses and hurl rocks at them. In this way we could do them more harm and hit them more often. Now Don Francisco was a small man, but the Turks recognized him as a leader by his armour and colourful trappings. While they were still in their boats they opened fire on him, and hit him with an arquebus shot. Luckily his breastplate was bullet-proof and he was unharmed. But soon after this, a Janissary, wearing a large black headdress with gold ornaments on it, knelt at the foot of the battery, aimed upwards at him and shot him in the groin. The bullet pierced the steel and he fell dead on the edge of the parapet. The Turks, seeing the knight fall, set up a shout of joy, as they always did when they killed any man of note.

Don Francisco was the first man to be killed at this post. I tried to recover his body, but could not do so because it was so very heavy. The attackers were so close to us at this point that they even tried to drag down the body from the parapet, pulling it by the legs, while we pulled by the arms. Finally we got the body away from them, but not before they had pulled off the shoes from his feet.

The death of Don Francisco de Sanoguera is mentioned by Balbi at some length, since he was captain of the post at which Balbi fought. But what must immediately strike the modern reader is the description of the weight of armour he was wearing. It does, indeed, remain one of the mysteries of this period (as well as of the Crusades) how men could fight under the midday sun of the near East in such heavy and unsuitable equipment. In mid-summer Malta it is common for the temperature to reach over ninety degrees, and in this heat a piece of metal soon becomes almost too hot to touch. Nevertheless the fact is that the knights did wear armour under these conditions, and there are numerous examples of it in the Royal Malta Museum. Sanoguera, we are told, was wearing a bullet-proof breastplate, and from specimens in existence we know that the average weight of one of these was about eighteen pounds, while a similar back-plate might weigh over twenty pounds. It was not the weight of the armour which must have been inconvenient, so much as the heat. A well-fitted suit of armour, such as the rich and noble Knights of St John

*will have worn, was constructed so that its weight was perfectly distributed
over his body. Except for the slowness of his movements, an armoured man
was hardly aware of the weight that he carried.*

After the death of Don Francisco, the Knight Adorno and Captain
Medrano's sergeant hastened to the post. The latter fought gallantly
throughout this action, even though he was suffering from a head
wound received at St Elmo. Others who should be signalled out for
mention were the clerk, Vincenzo Cigala, Mendoza, Lorenzo the
Mallorquin, and Master Juan Olivero. All these men were engaged
in the battle on the earthworks, where seven Turkish banners had
already been planted. The Turks by now had suffered immense
losses, for they came on heedless of danger since they felt it shameful
not to be able to take a place that looked so weak and vulnerable.
It was at this moment in the battle that the captains of reserves,
who had been standing by in Birgu, came over. Some of them went
straight to St Michael, while the rest came to the Spur, where they
were greatly needed and eagerly awaited.

Ten of the largest Turkish boats, seeing that the others which had
rowed against the chain defence were held up, and their men forced
to jump into the water, made straight for the very end of the Spur.
These large boats carried their very best troops. They could see no
chain at the end of the Spur, but they were unaware that the whole
of that part was dominated by the Post of Francisco de Guiral (the
battery on the water-level near the Great Chain). De Guiral, as soon
as he saw the boats, guessed their intention. He had all his guns
trained on them, but held his fire until exactly the right moment.
When he saw the boats nearing the land, and in a position where he
could not miss, he ordered a four- or five-gun salvo. Nine of the large
boats were immediately sunk, and not a man in them was saved.
Thus eight hundred Janissaries and Levantines were killed. The
guns of de Guiral's battery were not only loaded with shot, but fired
bags full of stones, pieces of chain, and iron caltrops.* It was these
which caused the carnage. Those of the men who were not killed or
wounded, were drowned. It is not surprising that, out of so many
troops, not one of them escaped, when one knows – as we learned

---

* The Spanish is 'abrojos d'hierro', literally 'thistles of iron'. I have rendered this by
the English 'caltrop' which the *O.E.D.* defines as a 'four-spiked iron ball thrown on
ground to maim cavalry horses'. It derives from the caltrop or star-thistle, and I have
no doubt that it was these four-spiked iron balls that de Guiral used with such
devastating effect.

afterwards – that the pashas had picked for this assault party all those who could not swim. The idea was that, not being able to save themselves in this way, they would make an even more determined landing.

To sum up this action, there can be no doubt that Commander de Guiral's battery saved the day. If these boats had landed and disembarked their troops, we should have been quite unable to resist them.

While this was going on, Marshal Melchior de Robles and all his knights and soldiers in St Michael were in the thick of the battle, for over eight thousand Turks attacked this post and that of Bormla. They met a resistance they had never expected, and not one of them managed to reach the top of the wall alive. The cross-fire from the Marshal's guns and the guns of Bormla was responsible for decimating the Turks attacking at this point. As soon as they saw the reinforcements under the Bailiff of the Eagle and Captain Romegas coming up, they started to retreat, first from St Michael and then from the Spur. In all, the attack had lasted five hours.

As soon as the Turks, who were on the shore, realized that their companions who had been attacking St Michael, were retreating, they wanted to follow suit. But they were unable to, for the boats from which they had disembarked had withdrawn and did not dare come back for them. Victory was now in our grasp, so we decided to sally out. The first men were Ramon, a Maltese; a Neapolitan; two Greeks, and myself. We ran out through a small gate which opens on to the shore, and using it as cover, we opened fire on the enemy. By now a number of other soldiers had dashed out and started to slaughter the Turks. Although a great many of them had been left behind on the shore, only four of them were spared and taken alive for questioning in front of the Grand Master.*

The Turkish gunners, seeing their men being butchered without mercy, opened fire on us and caused a number of casualties, for we were all out in the open. Their boats, unable to get near the shore, stood by not knowing what to do. It then appeared that they were about to embark more men and return to the attack, so the batteries on St Angelo, the windmills, and the Spur, immediately opened fire on them, forcing them to retreat out of range.

As I have said, the attack went on for five hours and by the time

* Other commentators state that the Maltese also sallied out and refused to take any prisoners – shouting as they killed the enemy: 'St Elmo's pay', in other words, no quarter, just as you showed no quarter to the garrison of St Elmo. The expression is used to this day in Malta for any engagement in which no mercy is shown.

the Turks had withdrawn they had lost about four thousand men, including those who were drowned. Our losses were two hundred dead and a great many wounded. We had captured six standards (those which had been planted on the earthworks) as well as many scimitars, arquebuses, bows, and a lot of money – some Turkish, and the rest of it Christian money which had been captured at St Elmo. But the people who did best were those who knew how to swim, for they secured a lot of loot out of the water. We found many documents in the purses of the dead Turks, as well as a great deal of hashish. In the sunken boats there was plenty of biscuit, barrels of water, raisins, sugar, honey, butter, and other foodstuffs. This was a clear sign that if they had captured the Spur they would have occupied it and stayed there.

Now that the assault was over, we gave thanks to God for his infinite mercy, and were led in our prayers by our preacher, Fra Roberto. During the attack Fra Roberto went to all the various posts, crucifix in one hand and a sword in the other, encouraging us to fight for the Faith of Jesus Christ and to die well. During this day's action, good Father Roberto was among those wounded. Now that the battle was over, the Grand Master had the captured standards laid in the Church of St Lawrence with great rejoicing, and with the singing of a solemn *Te Deum*. We began to recover and bury our many dead, and a great number of knights were among them. There was Don Francisco de Sanoguera, his nephew, Don Jaime, and Don Fadrique de Toledo, a son of Don Garcia.* He and Don Jaime had been standing together, talking, when a cannon shot killed them both. It was most tragic to see those two young and high-spirited knights laid dead. The Posts of the Spur and Bormla were now without captains, so La Valette put Claramonte in charge of the one, and Don Bernardo de Cabrera in charge of the other. The latter was now restored to health after the wounds he had received in St Elmo.

The whole of that night was spent in repairing the places that were the most threatened. We did not, in fact, expect another major assault after all the losses that the Turks had suffered, but we did fear a surprise attack. And indeed that very night despite their disastrous day, they did go down into the ditch of St Michael. There they dug trenches at the point where the barrels of earth were standing. In order to take cover from the fire of Martello's casemate they started to take stones out of the far side of the ravelin and the wall,

* He was an illegitimate son.

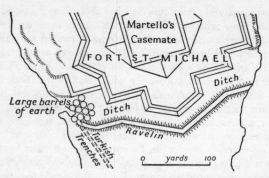

where they made themselves a number of shelters. This would also serve as a protection against the heat of the day and the damp of the night. From here they kept up a dangerous fire on all who showed themselves at the marshal's post.

IX

THE NEVER-ENDING BOMBARDMENT
OF ST MICHAEL CONTINUES AND
THERE IS NO SIGN OF FURTHER
RELIEF

Monday, 16 July. A violent frontal bombardment of St Michael began, while the fortifications from Corradino to Bormla also came under fire. The Spur was not attacked, so we concluded that the Turks had no intention of making another sea-borne assault. A few days later this was confirmed, for we saw them taking their boats back overland to Marsamuscetto.

Although the enemy bombardment kept up overnight, Marshal Robles sent out a party of men by the embrasure to make their way to the barrels. After a bitter struggle, the Turks finally retired, and our men thereupon destroyed the barrels. They then made their way down into the ditch but found no enemy, for they had already retired to their trenches on the other side. Our men took good note of the shelters the Turks had built, and even found some clothes in them.

Tuesday, 17 July. There was a heavy general bombardment, and we were kept busy repairing the defences. Since the battery sited at the Mandra kept up its frontal bombardment of St Michael, some of our guns were put out of action and part of the battlements collapsed into the ditch. Marshal Robles accordingly had our guns withdrawn to a more secure position. He also had a parapet erected of boards backed by earth, and behind it a stone wall shaped like a half moon. This was as tall as a man, ten feet thick, and pierced with plenty of loopholes. All of this work took place under very heavy fire.

The enemy now began building a bridge on five spans, designed to cross the ditch of St Michael, in front of the post which had been commanded by Hasdrubal de Medici. He had been killed, and his place was now taken by the Florentine knight, Martello. The sentries on this post saw what was happening, and Martello had a sally-port made ready so that, when the time was ripe, they could rush out to destroy the bridge.

Wednesday, 18 July. Already the five spans of the bridge were in position, so Commander Parisot, a nephew of the Grand Master, wanting to distinguish himself, went out with a number of soldiers to try to destroy it. The men who went out with him, as well as our sentries who watched him from above, maintained that instead of going out stealthily he made a great deal of noise. The result was that the Turks leapt up from their trenches and, when they saw what our men were doing, opened a heavy arquebus fire. Now Commander Parisot was dressed in rich armour inlaid with gold, which marked him out as someone of importance, so the Turks concentrated their fire on him. He was immediately killed, and the men who had gone out with him retreated from the ditch without having achieved anything.

The enemy had not concentrated solely on this one position, but were engaged in preparing numerous places from which to attack us. Today, for instance, their engineers were selecting a site for a further large gun platform on Mount Salvador. This seemed confirmation enough of the story we had heard from renegades, that the Turks intended to direct their maximum fire against the Post of Castile, as they had been advised to do by the slave from Captain Romegas' galley. As soon as he saw what they were planning, La Valette made haste to have the inner defences of Castile and Germany completed. Work was never ending in St Michael and the Post of Bormla, to ensure that the two traverses (each side of the Post of Don Bernardo de Cabrera) were made secure. This work was so well and so quickly finished that the post was soon inflicting great casualties on the enemy.

During the night some troops sent out by Captain Martello to fire the bridge, found it completely covered with damp soil. As a result it was necessary to use picks and shovels to dig a trench up to it. With the enemy artillery fire and the fighting which went on all night, these men were in a very dangerous position. However, under cover from the trench that they had dug, they managed to reach the woodwork of the bridge. They bound tow all round it, brought up pitch and other combustibles, and then set the whole lot on fire. They threw on all the inflammable material they could find, so that the bridge was destroyed and only one of its five spans was left. It was during this same night's action that Marshal Robles learned that the enemy was mining towards his post. Our men probed forward with a counter-mine and ran into the Turks. They killed all the Turkish miners, and the Marshal then had the mouth of the mine closed, mounting a guard of arquebusiers on it.

THE SIEGE OF ST MICHAEL

a. Fort St Angelo: b. Birgu: c. The Post of Provence: d. Mount Salvador: e. The chain: f. Manoel Island: g. The windmills: h. St Elmo captured by the Turks: i. The walls of St Michael: k. The galleon captured from the Turks: l. The bridge linking Birgu and the

island: m. The second chain: n. Arquebusiers on the scarp of the ditch: o. Artillery being transported from St Elmo: p. A battery bombarding Birgu and St Angelo: q. Dragut Point: r. Santa Margarita: s. Corradino Heights: t. Bormla: v. The Mandra: x. Boats being transported overland: y. A battery bombarding St Michael: z. The Turkish armada in Marsamuscetto.

Thursday, 19 July. The enemy were now in possession of the entrance to the ditch of St Michael on the Corradino side. From this position they were under cover from the guns of the casemate, and they now began digging a trench down to the sea. This was an immensely difficult task for they had to excavate solid rock. But all the same, within a few days, they had extended it beyond the post of Marshal Robles, and were very close to Bormla. This trench was a hundred and fifty paces long, and forty paces away from our walls. We could even hear the noise the rocks we hurled at them made on their wooden shields. As soon as they had finished this trench they, as usual, planted innumerable small flags along it – looking rather like handkerchiefs.

Friday, 20 July. The enemy was as busy as ever, building gun platforms on Mount Salvador. They now began erecting a stone wall from here to the sea, and they stationed arquebusiers along it, so as to return the fire of our men who were shooting at their workmen.

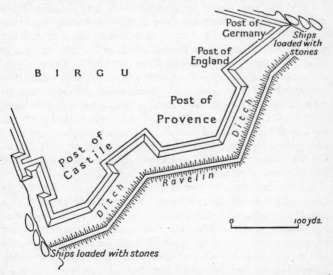

Now there were two most important positions at the Post of Castile, one the cavalier at the end, and the other a casemate close to the Post of Germany. This casemate had a great many traverses, some high and some low, which covered the curtain walls of the Posts of Germany and England, as well as the end of the cavalier.

After the death of Commander Paz, the latter had been put in the charge of Captain Buoninsegna. The Captain was a knight of the Order and a man who had served his Majesty the King in many an action. Don Rodrigo Maldonado, another knight of the Order, was in charge of the casemate.

Seeing the way things were going on Mount Salvador, La Valette felt sure that the Turks were going to launch a major offensive against the Post of Castile, attacking both by land and sea. To try and ward off any sea-borne assault, he had ships loaded with stones brought from the harbour by night and scuttled in front of the defences between the Posts of Germany and Castile. They were sunk ten or twelve paces beyond the walls, where we could easily see them, each ship being secured to the other. The Grand Master chose the largest ships, and heavy anchors secured to them by chains were laid ten paces away. This excellent and ingenious defence put an end to the fear of any attack by sea.

La Valette now turned his attention to the land defences. There were a number of houses that the enemy bombardment would inevitably destroy, so he had them immediately demolished. They were all built of large stone blocks, which he had broken up into small pieces, just the right size for throwing. He had a large supply of these put at all the exposed positions, and when the time came they proved as useful as any other kind of ammunition. All the defences by the outer ditch of Castile and Germany, the casemates, and the inner ring of defences were swiftly completed on his orders. Here as always, the Grand Master showed himself conscientious, vigilant, and ever-courageous. No one ever saw him show the slightest trace of fear. On the contrary, his presence was enough to inspire and put heart into knights and soldiers alike.

Meanwhile the commander in charge of the ammunition supply made sure that everything necessary was got ready as quickly as possible – gunpowder, cannon balls, grape-shot, incendiaries, fire-hoops, trumps, and sacks stuffed with cotton. The last of these was yet another invention of the Grand Master, the sacks being coated on the outside with pitch and filled with cotton and gunpowder. Even when the powder had all been burned, they would keep on blazing away so long as the pitch lasted, and they proved a great hindrance to the attacking enemy. They had a further advantage in that they were quick to prepare, and we had a good store of cotton and pitch.*

* Cotton was widely grown in Malta, and was one of the island's major exports.

The Commander of the Arsenal also had various vessels broken up, and their timber used for making retaining walls and other similar defences. Among his duties was that of seeing that tarred hoops were prepared, as well as yarn and rope – materials which were mixed with wetted earth and served for repairs in place of brushwood bundles. He also had sacks made out of the cloaks of dead slaves and from old awnings, and these were then filled with earth. This was a very quick way of repairing fortifications, and indeed the only way in which we could have counteracted the enemy's bombardment, lasting, as it did, from eight to ten hours.

Thanks to the Grand Master's diligence and foresight all our defences were in as good a state as they could be. We anticipated a really heavy bombardment from all quarters, for the Turks were clearly preparing one. We could see that the gun-ports on their platforms – those that were detailed to be used against us – were, according to custom, distinguished by a flag. During this night they brought up all their artillery and laid it in position.

Sunday, 22 July. At dawn, fourteen batteries, composed of sixty-four heavy guns and four basilisks, opened fire on us. The shot fired by the basilisks was capable of pentrating twenty-one feet of earth. We had proof of this at the Post of Don Bernardo de Cabrera, where some of his soldiers were killed alongside him. When all of these guns fired simultaneously, the noise and the concussion was such that it seemed as if the end of the world was coming. To show you just how terrific the volume of noise was, it could be clearly heard in Syracuse and even in Catania, one hundred and twenty miles from Malta.

The Grand Master had heard that Don Garcia, although it had been against his orders, had approved of Don Juan de Cardona's action in landing his troops, and that he realized this relief was the salvation of the Order. But in view of the dangerous situation in which the Order stood, and that the relief sent was so small, Don Garcia decided to send off some more galleys on chance. With this in view, Don Juan de Sanoguera volunteered to take the risk in the service of God, his king, and the Order.

Now it happened that, while these preparations were being made, Giovanni Andrea Doria read some of the letters which had been received from the Grand Master, whom he held in great respect as his own Lord, as well as loving La Valette as if he had been his father. He was so moved when he read of the dire straits in which the Order and La Valette stood, that he went to Don Garcia and

offered to go down to Malta with three galleys, taking in them as
many troops as possible. His one stipulation was that all the oarsmen
should be Christians, and that they should be given their freedom
on arrival and arms with which to fight as soldiers. He wanted, he
said, no payment for his galleys, while he himself would supply the
stores. All he asked of Don Garcia was the two companies of
Spanish veterans from the garrison of Naples who were there [in
Messina], and permission to take with him all the gentlemen and
soldiers of fortune. He also asked that he might be allowed to choose
such men as he required from the troops of Pompeo Colonna. After
explaining the intention behind the expedition, he asked Don
Garcia to promise that if he, Andrea Doria, should be killed or
taken prisoner, Don Garcia would see that his heirs paid his debts
out of his estates.

Andrea Doria's offer seemed reasonable to Don Garcia and,
despite some opposition, preparations were set on foot. The gentlemen and soldiers of fortune were already mustered when Don
Garcia changed his mind. He felt that he could not spare Andrea
Doria. Furthermore, Pompeo Colonna was a very important knight
in command of the papal troops, and he had already offered to go
to the relief with his own men. Pompeo Colonna protested, with
the result that Don Garcia ordered Monsieur de Leyni, Captain of
Savoy, to go with his galleys as far as the entrance to Grand Harbour. Two of the galleys were to be those of the Order, and one of
them from the king's ships under the command of Don Juan de
Sanoguera. Don Garcia wrote accordingly to the Grand Master
telling him that this expedition was being prepared. He said that,
should the troops break through successfully, La Valette was to
signal to Leyni so that the latter could bring him the news.

These galleys did in fact come to Malta, but they never entered
the harbour. Rumour has it that they were never given the signal to
do so, because La Valette knew about the enemy shipping at the
mouth of Grand Harbour, and was not willing to hazard the galleys
of the relief force.

*Balbi's involved account of the political machinations in Sicily must not be
considered absolutely reliable, for he was only an ordinary arquebusier and had
no knowledge of what went on in the councils of the great. The Giovanni
Andrea Doria who is mentioned by Balbi was a nephew of the famous
Admiral, Andrea Doria. During the great debate in Messina, on the question
of whether relief should be sent to Malta or not, Giovanni Andrea Doria*

was the leader of what may be called the 'War Party'. He was in favour of taking his own galleys and whatever others and troops he could muster, at his own expense and sailing straight for Malta. The opposing party, who had great influence over Don Garcia, did everything that they could to obstruct the relief of Malta. Personal rivalries, no doubt, came into this, but above all there was always a certain jealousy of the Order on the part of the rich and powerful who did not belong to it. This was largely due to the Order's aristocratic exclusiveness, and partly to the fact that in a century when national wars were absorbing Europe, an international force like that of the Order was not only an anachronism, but even seemed dangerous to many of the European rulers.

The party who were against going to the relief of Malta maintained that La Valette should accept terms from the Turks – just as Villiers de L'Isle Adam had done at Rhodes. They saw no reason why they should hazard themselves, their ships or their fortunes, to save this exclusive and arrogant Order, which had often 'black-balled' their own sons.

Two other small points may serve to clarify Balbi's diary entry for 22 July. Giovanni Andrea Doria asked that all his oarsmen should be Christians. While many of the oarsmen in the galleys of the period were Turkish slaves, Christians were also sent to them to serve jail sentences. Debtors were also able to discharge their obligations by signing on as oarsmen for a necessary period of time, their pay being automatically handed over to their creditors. Secondly, as Balbi rightly supposes, the galleys under de Leyni never landed their troops. La Valette never gave the necessary signal. The mouth of Grand Harbour was swarming with Piali's ships, and no galleys would have had a chance of bursting through the blockade. When the main relief force did finally arrive, it landed its troops at the far end of the island, away from the Turkish vessels on patrol off Grand Harbour.

The Turkish batteries were now so disposed that there were thirty-eight guns on Mount Salvador bombarding the Posts of Castile, Germany, Auvergne, and St Angelo. Twenty-six were trained on Castile, four on the two traverses of Auvergne, four on the Post of Germany, and four on St Angelo.

St Michael was under fire from six guns on Santa Margarita hill, six at the Mandra, and two on the high ground of Paulo Micho's vineyard. The Post of Marshal Robles and Fort St Michael both came under fire from six guns on Corradino. Also, at the far end of Corradino, there were two guns bombarding the Post of Bormla, commanded by Captain Don Bernardo de Cabrera. One of these two guns was a basilisk, and the other a reinforced cannon. They also bombarded the houses of Birgu. The battery on the promontory of St Elmo engaged the Post of Claramonte, which had formerly been that of Don Francisco de Sanoguera. The noise and concussion of all these guns was awe-inspiring, and there was not a single safe place anywhere in Birgu or in St Michael.

During this period of the siege, the cavalry in Mdina was not inactive, making constant excursions by day and night under the command of Monsieur Boisbreton and Vincenzo Anastasi. A typical incident was as follows. A Christian, who had escaped from the Turkish fleet, told us that the Turks led a party of six hundred other Christians out to fetch water every morning. The escort, he said, was no more than two hundred Turkish auxiliaries and a hundred men could easily rout them in a surprise attack, since they were second-line troops – and in this way rescue the Christians.

When they heard this, the cavalry commanders sallied out of Mdina at night and laid an ambush in a valley near the Marsa, at the place where the Turks used to go to fetch water. They posted scouts and waited. Now it happened that, on that particular day, the Turks did not arrive at the usual hour, but sent scouts out ahead of them before leaving the fleet. These were seen by our men and reported to Monsieur Boisbreton. He had also sent out an experienced Maltese to see what was going on at the Marsa, who returned with the news that a large and disciplined body was approaching. Now it was already daylight and, since our troops would soon be discovered, the cavalry commanders decided to attack. They charged the Turkish line furiously, broke it, and in this first attack killed over forty of the enemy. The Turks then formed up in a large body and prepared to give battle. At this, our cavalry commanders ordered the men who were badly mounted to retire to Mdina, while the others received the Turkish charge and held off the enemy. This they did with the loss of only one soldier, having killed more than sixty Turks in the engagement.

Monday, 23 July. On this day as on the previous, the Turkish bombardment was so rapid and concentrated that no one except an eye-witness could credit it. In addition, they made a great many night-alarms, some genuine and others false; sometimes making a reconnaissance and on other occasions improving their trenches. But, whatever it was, they always met with a stiff resistance.

One could no longer walk through any of the streets near the palace, for the Turks on Mount Salvador were too near. The Grand Master had the streets barricaded with stone walls, so that the enemy arquebusiers could not see if anyone was passing through them. At the same time, he made haste to have all the necessary repairs carried out, even though there were heavy casualties among the workmen, the overseers, and the engineers.

Tuesday, 24 July. The Grand Master's troubles increased. He was not only worried because the relief had not come, but also because he could get no news through from Mdina, since the Turks had occupied the paths by which messengers usually came. The enemy had also managed to capture one of our boats on its way over from Sicily, in which the captain was carrying dispatches in cipher. His name was Orlando, and he had with him George of Malvasia, a Greek who spoke Turkish fluently, and who had been sent by Don Garcia to act as a spy in the enemy camp. The intention was that he should then make his way to Mdina and pass on information to the governor, who would recognize him when he handed over the counter-sign – half a *scudo*. The governor would then have sent him back to Sicily to pass on his news to Don Garcia. Such was the scheme that had been worked out, but the boat was captured in the Malta–Gozo channel and all its crew taken before the pasha. We heard from renegades that the pasha was mad with rage because there was no one in all his army or fleet who could decipher the dispatches. We also heard that Captain Orlando and George the Greek said that Don Garcia had one hundred galleys, sixty merchant

ships, and fifty other vessels between Messina and Syracuse. The
Turks were astounded at this news and asked if the King of France
or the Venetians had lent some galleys, or in other ways aided the
King of Spain. When they learned that this was not so, they
marvelled even more at the great power of this king.

One night about this time, the Turks brought Orlando to the
trenches in front of Provence. He was in chains, and had been told
by his captors exactly what he should say. The Turks called out to
the sentries on guard, telling them to rouse the Grand Master, for
Orlando wished to talk to him. La Valette, having found out what
was going on, went to the place in person, but did not reveal who he
was. The Bailiff of the Eagle called out to Orlando: 'Say what you
have to say to me, for the Grand Master will not come.' Orlando then
began to extol the might of the Turks, and to denigrate the forces
of the Grand Master. He said also that the relief that they were
expecting from Sicily was a joke – there were only fifty galleys and
they were poorly equipped. 'They will never dare', he said, 'face a
fleet as powerful as that of the Turks, which is strong enough to
attack Sicily itself, let alone to take a little place like Malta, weak and
undefended as it is.' He continued by saying that the pashas knew
all about our losses and the dire straits we were in, and that was why
they advised the Grand Master to surrender to the sultan. They
would give him the best possible terms, and they only made this offer
to avoid a repetition of St Elmo. If the Grand Master let obstinacy
rule him rather than reason, the same thing was bound to happen,
while if he delayed in making up his mind whether to accept this
offer, he would find it useless to ask for similar terms at a later date.

It was clear to our people, judging by the interval between one
sentence and another, that Orlando was being prompted by the
Turks as to what he should say. The Grand Master replied: 'Orlando,
you have risen a long way from a simple sailor, that you are now an
ambassador! However, if the Turks are prepared, I will ransom
you.' But they replied that the pashas would not let him go for any
amount of money. Whereupon the Grand Master gave orders that
the Turks should be told to withdraw. He then had the arquebusiers
open fire in their direction so that they would not be able to take
advantage of the occasion by carrying out a reconnaissance in the
ditch of Provence and Auvergne. This was the only kind of reply
that they could have expected from so valiant a prince as La Valette.

Wednesday, 25 July. Since this was the feast of St James, we felt
convinced that relief would come, for St James is the patron saint of

Spain, while Don Garcia himself belonged to the Order of St James. But the day and the night passed, and no relief arrived. The Grand Master, who had maintained that we would surely be relieved on that day, not knowing what to say to put heart into the people, spoke out in public, maintaining that he hoped for no help save that of God. It was God who was our true relief, and He who had preserved us up to now, would certainly deliver us from the hands of the enemies of His Holy Faith. It was in God alone that we should put our trust. He did not know what to say about the promises of Don Garcia, since the time for their fulfilment was now past, but he asked every one of us to bear in mind that we were Christians. We were fighting above all for the faith of Our Lord Jesus Christ, and for our lives and liberty. Each one of us must remember that there was no hope of any more mercy from the Turks than had been shown to the defenders of St Elmo, and that in all our dangers we would always find him in the vanguard.

This speech of the Grand Master was soon known by everyone, and there was not a man who did not resolve to die rather than fall into the hands of the Turks. We were all determined to sell our lives dearly and to waste no more time in hoping for outside help. When he heard of our determination, La Valette was greatly pleased, although he had always had confidence in the spirit of his knights and soldiers. Wanting to let our resolution be known to those in Mdina, La Valette took advantage of the fact that on 27 June the chain with which the enemy sealed the mouth of Grand Harbour had been broken in a storm, and sent out a messenger with the news.*

From 22 July onwards (when they began their general bombardment) the Turks kept up a continuous fire until the 27th. During this period there were a thousand alarms and excursions, as well as a number of attacks which caused us great anxiety, since both St Michael and the Post of Castile had been practically levelled to the ground. But in a way this was to our advantage since the Turks could not make a mass assault owing to the constricted space,† and

* This is the first mention we have of any chain sealing off Grand Harbour. It would probably have been laid shortly after the Turkish capture of St Elmo, and would have run between the end of the peninsula on which St Elmo stands and Gallows Point. Equally, although there was no longer any communication overland, it will always remain a mystery how Piali's fleet could have been so lax as to let a messenger and a boat get out of Grand Harbour.

† What Balbi means by this is that the debris from the crumbling walls prevented the Turks from advancing *en masse* since it had spilled outwards and made, as it were, a corridor flanked by piles of rubble.

were forced to advance two abreast. Another point in our favour
was that, in order to attack the Post of Castile, they had to cross a
narrow neck of water.

Seeing the damage that was being wrought on the Post of Castile
by the enemy gunfire, the Grand Master, brave and vigilant as
always, left the house in which he had been living, and made his
headquarters in a merchant's shop in the main square. He did this
so that he could always be ready to give help wherever it was needed,
and because all the reserves were accustomed to gather in the square,
and from here he could quickly dispatch them wherever the need was
greatest. He also gave orders that the morning *Angelus* should be
rung two hours before daybreak, and not one hour before as
normally. At the same time drums were to beat at all the posts
calling the men to their stations, and as soon as this was over, the
bell in the main square was to sound the alarm. The Grand Master
took all these precautions, although the enemy made no move as
yet, for he knew how useful they would be in the event of an attack
– which the rules of war made inevitable.* This training also made
sure that the men would not be caught out at any time but would
learn to go to their posts at the double, so that when the need really
arose, troops who were slow by nature would have grown accustomed to move quickly. The Turks, for their part, were both
astonished and downhearted by the evidence of our efficiency and
alertness.

Whenever the Grand Master went to the square, sometimes alone
and sometimes accompanied, two pages were always at his side.
One carried his helmet and shield and the other a pike. With the
Grand Master were usually to be found the Bailiff of the Eagle
(until he was killed), Marshal Robles, Conservator La Motta,
Commander Saquavilla, and Romegas. Also in his company was
a jester who had come to the island with Marshal Robles. During
the Turkish attacks he kept La Valette informed of what was
happening at the various posts, as well as trying to amuse him with
his quips – although there was little enough to laugh about.

---

* The 'rules of war', to which Balbi refers, were the normally accepted code for the
conduct of siege warfare. Under this code, once a large breach had been made in the
walls, the main assault must inevitably take place. If the siege was being conducted
chivalrously – which was not the case in Malta – the defenders of a breached position
might normally come to terms with the attackers. If, however, they refused to 'concede
the game' after the breach was made, they had no right to expect any mercy. In Malta,
of course, it had already been established that no quarter was being given.

On many an occasion the enemy tried to make a silent assault, but as soon as they were discovered the bell was rung. This forced them to retreat before they ever launched their attack, for they realized that we were on the alert and always expecting them. But, despite the fact that our defences were very weak from the bombardment, the Turks showed no great heart in their attempts to attack us. They had learned their lesson from the immense losses they had suffered in the past.

Friday, 27 July. The Turkish guns had been silent throughout the night, but opened up in the morning in a heavy bombardment which lasted until noon. At this hour, thinking that the garrison of St Michael would be taking their meal, about two hundred Turks brought up sandbags and planks for a reconnaissance expedition. Our sentries saw them and the general alarm was sounded. The Turks, moving from trench to trench, got right up to the Post of Bormla, at which point they came under a heavy fire of incendiaries. This caused one of their powder flasks to explode, which, in its turn, set fire to others causing over thirty casualties. The rest fled, without having achieved anything.

Saturday, 28 July. St Michael being so badly battered, and the Turkish trenches being so near the walls, we had scouts posted almost outside the defences, less than twenty paces from the enemy. During the day, one of the scouts on duty, a young Maltese – either because he was asleep or caught by surprise – was captured and had his head cut off before the alarm could be given. Over a thousand Turks armed with scimitars, shields, and incendiaries, now attacked the whole of the marshal's post. They hoped to do as they had done against the ravelin of St Elmo, but they were thwarted. The post was so well defended that the Turks were forced to retire. They came back to the attack four times in all, and lost one hundred men. Our casualties were six Maltese soldiers and Filippo Doria, a knight of the Order.

The night was fraught with suspense. The never-ending bombardment of Castile and the houses near by continued. We suffered great casualties among the people working on the defences, and a great many women and children were also killed in the houses. The reason the Turks were able to bring such effective fire to bear on this quarter was because the Posts of Buoninsegna and Don Rodrigo Maldonado, and the curtain-wall between them, had been so badly damaged. Also, they were continually shifting their guns from one place to another, so that we could not get a bearing on them.

X

FURTHER ATTACKS ARE BEATEN OFF
BUT A SPANISH SOLDIER DESERTS

Saturday, 28 July to *Monday, 30 July*. Throughout these three days the Turkish bombardment was continuous. It was concentrated on St Michael, where the defences were so bad that nothing separated us from the Turks but a few barrels filled with earth. The Grand Master was gravely concerned about this, particularly as the expected assault never came. It was by the Grace of God that we discovered the ruse with which the Turks intended to take St Michael on their first assault. If we had not found it out, the position would certainly have been lost, and once that had happened Birgu could not have held out for long.

Despite their continual and intensive bombardment, the enemy's intention was to take St Michael by surprise, without making any initial assault. I have already explained how the enemy had got themselves established in the ditch of St Michael, shielded from the

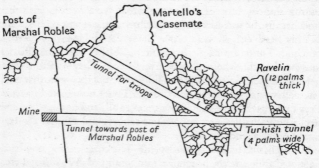

guns of Martello by means of the shelters they had made. They excavated one of these shelters until they were right up to the wall at its most damaged point, where the ravelin was serving as a parapet. Having got this far, they started to take away the stones from the ravelin, which was twelve palms thick. They then began to cut a way through it, along its length, in order to reach the top of the fort. They dug a tunnel four palms wide, that is to say leaving four palms' thickness of wall on either side. They worked on it only during the daylight, and kept up a heavy bombardment so that the noise of their sappers could not be discovered. This tunnel when we came upon it, was nearly completed.

Using the same entrance, they dug another tunnel towards the Post of Marshal Robles. Having got beneath it without being discovered, they made ready a mine and were about to fill it with gunpowder. Their intention was to make an assault, and when the defenders were all manning the walls along that section, they would blow up the mine. This was certain to cause heavy casualties and considerable confusion, and at that moment the men who were in the tunnel were to burst into the fort and shoot down the survivors from their position above them. The bulk of the Turkish army would storm the batteries, and St Michael would fall.

In order to carry out this plan, the Aga of the Janissaries asked Marshal Robles to a parley. In fact, he had nothing to say to him, but as he was within earshot, the Marshal told him to say whatever he had to as quickly as possible. The aga thereupon replied that his business was a matter entrusted to him by the pashas, and that it would take at least two hours. The marshal immediately replied that he had no wish for such a long interview, and ordered him to retire before he was fired upon. He even had some incendiaries thrown in his direction to force him to retreat. The Turkish plan was that, while the aga was holding the marshal in conversation, their men should enter the tunnel and make the final adjustments to the mine which was due to go up the same day. But, by the will of God, while their engineers were inside trying to find out how close they were to the surface, they began probing with a spear. Now the earth was so loose owing to the concussions of the bombardment, that with the movement of the spear it all began to slide. One of our Spanish sentries noticed this and immediately reported to Marshal Robles. He sent his ensign, Andreas de Muñatones, to investigate, who at once saw the tip of the spear protruding, and called up men with picks and shovels to start digging to the right of it. It was not long before they found the exit of the tunnel, and Muñatones immediately threw an incendiary down it. Then with great courage, he himself dashed down into the tunnel, followed by two knights armed with swords and shields. Three Spanish arquebusiers showed equal courage and followed them.

The Turks, realizing that they were discovered, and that our soldiers were hot on their heels, immediately fled – but not before some of them had been wounded in their dash for safety. Muñatones, and a number of knights and soldiers, now reached the mouth of the tunnel and saw what peril we had been in. They also found the mine which was already right under the Post of Marshal Robles. There was no one in it, however, for the Turks had all taken to their heels as soon as they heard the noise.*

Ensign Muñatones now had masons seal off the main entrance to these mines with solid blocks of stone. At the same time they left a number of loopholes for muskets so that we could fire on the enemy, as well as keeping them under observation. The Grand Master, overjoyed at the miraculous way at which we had been delivered from disaster, went and gave thanks to God as indeed he always did. For often he went alone to the Church of St Lawrence and said his prayers, something that he never neglected to do whenever he had a moment to spare. In recognition of the bravery of Ensign Muñatones, and as a reward for his service to the Order, our revered Grand Master presented him with a golden chain, worth three hundred *scudi*. To make the distinction even more notable, the chain was presented to him by Commander Buoninsegna, La Valette sending him a message to the effect that the chain was not so much a reward, as a token of his goodwill. He knew that the ensign would continue his faithful service, and he had every hope that God, in due course, would give the Grand Master the opportunity to reward him as he truly deserved. The other knights and soldiers received the Grand Master's thanks for all that they had done, the soldiers being rewarded with some ducats.

The admiral, Pedro de Monte, now fell ill owing to his ceaseless exertions as well as to his age, and he retired to the Auberge of Italy in Birgu. Commander Pedro Giustiniano, his lieutenant, remained in St Michael throughout the siege, while Carlo Scaravello took charge of the incendiary supplies and proved extremely efficient in his duties.

La Valette, seeing that the position of St Michael grew worse from hour to hour, withdrew a great many of the knights of all Langues from their posts, and sent them over to St Michael. Along with them, as captain of the reserves, went Don Vincenzo Caraffa, the Prior of Hungary, who took over the position between Marshal Robles and Don Carlo Rufo.

* Presumably the Turkish sapping party who were working on this mine-head had time to run out and escape after Muñatones had thrown down his incendiary, and before he and the others had dashed down the tunnel.

Tuesday, 31 July. After the discovery of their mines, the Turks recommenced a very heavy bombardment, causing great damage to the houses. During this day, however, they did not fire on our batteries, so we lost no time in repairing them. Although the Grand Master did all that he could for the safety of the women and children, and ordered them to take shelter in the safest parts (there were few enough of them), nevertheless many of them perished in the ruins of their houses. Every day, seeing that the noose grew tighter around us, the Grand Master must surely have been gravely disturbed, for he received no news, nor could he send out any on his own account. What was more, the Turks began to rebuild the bridge by the Post of Antonio Martello. They soon abandoned it however, possibly thinking that they could never use it. The men working on repairing the defences throughout St Michael were in full view of the enemy, and consequently suffered heavy losses from their gunfire. The marshal, in order to reduce the casualties, had ships' sails spread out in various places, not as a protection, but to prevent the Turks from being able to see what they were shooting at. This was most successful, because they were only able to fire at random.

Wednesday, 1 August. The bombardment kept up, but without any specific targets. Sometimes the Turks would open fire on the batteries, sometimes on the houses, and occasionally they even fired into the air – as if to show us that they could afford to waste ammunition. During the night, by God's good Grace, a man managed to get through to our lines with a message from the Governor of Mdina. He said that the cavalry had captured some Turks, from whom they had learned that there would be a general assault on St Michael on 2 August. He warned us to be ready for it, and the Grand Master at once informed Marshal Robles and the other captains, so that they were on the alert.

Thursday, 2 August. The bombardment kept up until noon, and then the Turks immediately launched their assault. The battle was fought with the utmost courage by friend and foe alike. The Posts of Marshal Robles and of Don Carlo Rufo bore the brunt, both of them being repeatedly attacked by wave upon wave of fresh troops for four hours. On the orders of La Valette, these two posts were reinforced by the Captains from other posts in St Michael, and their troops.

It was after about five hours' fighting that some twenty Turks managed to get up on to the Post of Marshal Robles; seeing this, he and his ensign, Muñatones, dashed at them with incendiaries. They were followed by three arquebusiers, and between them, so great was their courage, they forced the Turks to retire with many casualties. Throughout this action the Turkish artillery kept firing, but only blank-shot. The Turks, of course, knew about this, which was the reason that they had climbed up the walls, but our men for their part did not realize it to begin with, and dared not show themselves. As soon as they discovered the trick, however, they came out from under cover. After a hard fight that lasted all of five hours, the Turks began to withdraw, having lost over six hundred of their finest fighting men. We lost forty of our best soldiers of all nationalities, and a great many wounded. Most of our casualties were caused by their artillery, for whenever they saw our men out in the open they bombarded furiously.

After the Turks had completed their withdrawal, Marshal Robles fell on his knees, giving thanks to God for the successful conclusion of the action. In front of all the troops who stood round about, he called over to him three arquebusiers and said: 'Gentlemen, here and before God, I award you ten extra *scudi*, for I saw your actions today and, if Don Garcia should not be prepared to pay it, then I promise, if I live, that I will pay it myself. But I have faith in the munificence of our king who, when he hears of your valour, will not only confirm my award, but will increase it.'

Throughout the rest of the day and the night that followed, the enemy kept up their bombardment. Not content with this, but in order to reduce our morale, they daily dug new trenches so that soon there wasn't a single stone in the area that had not been shifted – notwithstanding the fact that there is nothing more abundant in Malta than stones, since every field is separated from its neighbour by dry stone walls. These stones the enemy used to make cover for themselves against our arquebusiers.

Grand Master La Valette, indomitable though his spirit was, was sorely tried (not without good reason), yet he concealed his feelings with his usual wisdom. The thing that distressed him most was that he had no news from Don Garcia, and that he had no idea as to what the enemy's intentions were. Neither by land nor by sea could he send out any messengers, for the Turks had by now repaired the chain at the mouth of Grand Harbour (which had been broken in the storm), while on the landward side we were completely surrounded.

Although our defences were crumbling, and the Turkish trenches were so close to them, he had it publicly proclaimed that any soldier who captured a Turk alive, should, apart from the honour he earned thereby, be given fifty *scudi*. He did this in the hope of gaining some information about the enemy's plans. Now Commander Romegas, distressed by La Valette's anxiety and wanting to afford him some relief, dispatched a small armed boat overnight in the direction of the harbour mouth. He ordered the men in it to take up station near Rinella Point, since this was the place where the Turks landed on their way from the fleet to the trenches and gun platforms on Salvador. Their orders were to try and capture a Turk alive. The boat accordingly went out and was quite close to Rinella when a Turkish brigantine drew near them. Not only were they forced to alter course but, in order to escape, all the crew had to jump into the sea. The night being dark and the men all good swimmers, they managed to get away but lost their boat and all their arms.

Romegas, seeing that he had failed by sea, decided to try again by land. He was proud of his men, and in order to encourage them, offered one hundred *scudi* out of his own pocket over and above the reward promised by the Grand Master – to any man who could capture a Turk alive out of the trenches. So great was his wish to help the Grand Master that, if the latter had allowed it, he himself would have gone out alone on this mission. He was quite well aware of the dangers he would run, for though others might be taken prisoner by the enemy, Romegas would rather die than have that happen. His soldiers, understanding their captain's wishes, determined to go out and see what they could do.

Friday, 3 August. It was on this night that Romegas' men went out by the casemate of Auvergne into the ditch of Provence, at a point where there was a defensive bridge running up to the top of the ditch. Once they were up there, they made straight for the nearest trenches, but they found them deserted. The enemy stationed in them had retreated into the guardposts of the bastion when they heard our men coming. Their mission was therefore fruitless, and indeed all they had achieved was to cause the Turks to keep a careful watch over this area. La Valette was greatly disheartened, for he had had great hopes of success, and Romegas was equally downcast.

Juan Vazquez de Aviles, seeing that the Grand Master had not got what he wanted, asked permission to go out himself, although he had been ill and was not yet recovered. He begged the Grand Master for permission to go, to such effect that the latter agreed, telling him to take as many men as he wanted. Accordingly, during the second watch of the night, he went out with fifty men of all nations.

Saturday, 4 August. And so in the early morning, Juan Vazquez de Aviles, Quincy, a serving brother and five other men, sallied out, thinking that the others were following them. They got right up to the trenches, but found that they were full of Turks. What was worse, forewarned by the events of the previous night, the Turkish guard had been doubled and men had been posted in concealed positions. Juan Vazquez and the men with him rushed at the enemy, but soon found that they were alone and surrounded. They fought where they stood and died to a man. Waiting to see what happened, the Grand Master was standing on the Post of Castile, when the troops who had failed to follow Juan Vazquez returned. God knows the sorrow of the Grand Master when he saw that eight were missing from the party, and these the leaders – men from whom the Turks might extract information about the weakness of the defences. Juan Vazquez, in particular, knew all the secrets of the fortifications.

Sunday, 5 August. No sooner was the first light in the sky than we saw, above the main platform of Salvador, eight heads on the points of lances. These were the men who had been lost, and the heads of the two knights were set apart, above the others. The Grand Master knew then that they had kept their word, and had died rather than surrender.

After midday there was a steady bombardment, and then a great number of Turks bearing sacks of gunpowder launched an attack on St Michael. The fighting went on for at least two hours, at the end of which the Turks retreated having suffered heavily. We had lost one soldier killed, but no one was wounded. During the night, about the second watch, over six hundred enemy arquebusiers approached the trenches opposite Aragon, France, Provence, Auvergne, and Castile. From each trench they fired three rounds as fast as they could. They did this to let the Grand Master know that all their trenches were well-manned.

Monday, 6 August. This was the day when the devil tempted a Spanish soldier and led him to perdition, causing him to desert – notwithstanding the fact that he had a pretty young wife in Gozo, of good family, by whom he had children. As he was a trained soldier of good reputation, he did not want to carry out his evil intention without giving some apparent reason for going out of the fortress. The way in which he contrived to do so I was told by José Castellon, a Catalan gentleman, who served throughout the siege either as one of the garrison or among the reserves.

The name of the Spanish soldier was Francisco de Aguilar, and he served under Commander de Guiral. Now, the captain's table-servant was in the habit of giving Aguilar whatever he asked for from the captain's table, and it happened that one day Aguilar asked for a delicacy not obtainable during the siege. The man-servant told him that he had not got it, and Aguilar, in return, abused him and even assaulted him. When the captain heard of this, being a gentleman and not wanting to lose his temper, he sent word that Aguilar should be barred from coming to his post any more, so that the Grand Master should be spared any petty cause of worry.

Now although the man had been told not to come into the presence of Captain de Guiral any further, he nevertheless presented himself at the post – for he was looking for an excuse for his treachery. As soon as the captain saw him, he was infuriated by the man's disobedience and, losing his temper, gave him a good piece of his mind. Francisco de Aguilar, pretending to be very hurt, went to St Michael and told the marshal the story of what had happened, as though seeking redress. Now the marshal, having seen Aguilar conduct himself well in a number of engagements, was impressed by his speech and appearance and ordered him to stay with his troops. He said that he himself would look after Aguilar, if he proved himself as good a soldier as he believed him to be.

As a result, Aguilar was sometimes with the marshal when our situation – whatever it might be – was being discussed, and at other times he would be with the Grand Master. He even went to the palace, and into the very room where our leaders discussed their plans, and heard all that was said. Since he was believed to be a good and trustworthy soldier there was no reason why he should have been told to withdraw. Then, at other times, he would visit the various posts, and since he was experienced, he could not fail to note our weaknesses and shortage of troops. Not content with all this, he often asked Bajada to tell him how he managed to get back and forth between Mdina and Birgu, what route he took, and if he ever came across the enemy.* Bajada answered that if he did not know him to be a good man and an honest soldier, he would have reported him to the Grand Master, for he asked things that no one had a right to know – things of such very great importance, that no one outside

---

* Balbi has previously stated that all routes out of the besieged positions were blocked and that La Valette was no longer able to communicate with Mdina, and via Mdina with Sicily. Presumably the traitor Aguilar did not know this. Bajada, of course, normally served as the messenger between Birgu and Mdina, and was to do so again at a later stage in the siege.

the council ought to be acquainted with them. Seeing that he had somewhat aroused Bajada's suspicions, Francisco de Aguilar asked no more. He already knew everything that he wanted to, and being determined to carry out his vile plan, he went ahead as follows.

On the 6th, during the dinner hour he went to the Post of Provence, with his arquebus on his shoulder and wearing his plumed helmet.* He went down to the casemate, and stayed there quite a time, talking with the soldiers he knew, who were on guard duty. As soon as he felt that all was safe he lit the slow-match of his musket and went over to the embrasure of Aragon, saying 'I can't see any of these curs!', to give the impression that he was eager to have a shot at the enemy. He stayed like this for a time, and then, picking his moment, leapt out of the embrasure into the ditch. He dashed along it at full speed, past the Post of Aragon, towards the Turkish trenches at Bormla. As he jumped, the soldiers gave the alarm. They opened fire on him from the Posts of Provence, France, Aragon, and St Michael. However, God permitted him to get through without being hit. When he reached the Turkish advance trenches, he was received with great rejoicing. They took him over to Kalkara where Mustapha Pasha had his tent, and there can be no doubt that the pasha must have been delighted to learn how the Grand Master and the people in Birgu were suffering.

This very same night, the Grand Master, who would not yield to anyone in the matter of bravado – for whatever the Turks did, he always answered them with a larger gesture, and planned his replies in such a way that the enemy never knew what to expect – acted as follows. Because on the night prior to Aguilar's desertion the Turks had fired salvos from all their trenches, he now had all the arquebusiers and every man who knew how to handle a gun, man the defences of Birgu, St Michael, and St Angelo. About an hour after dark he had them open fire with such rapidity that it seemed as if the whole place was ablaze. We loaded and fired four volleys to give the enemy the impression that we had plenty of troops, for our fire was such that it seemed as if five thousand arquebusiers were in action. As the Turks were in the habit of shouting out to us every day that we had hardly any men, La Valette, in order to disillusion them (or rather to fill them full of illusions), gave orders that arquebuses should be handed out from the armoury to all those who had not got one.

When the Turkish dogs observed our fire, they sent up a shout of

* The plumed Spanish-style casque such as the arquebusiers all wore.

derision. However, we soon learned from renegades that they were alarmed to see so much arquebus-fire, having been under the impression that we had not enough men to man the walls.

The pashas' joy at the desertion of de Aguilar was as great as the Grand Master's distress, for La Valette knew well that, besides being a good soldier, de Aguilar was also very well informed. Bajada also told the Grand Master what had taken place between him and de Aguilar. La Valette had good reason to believe, as indeed it proved, that the deserter would not only reveal our plight, but would also tell the pashas how determined we were to die rather than to surrender.

Since all our defences were so dangerously reduced, La Valette foresaw that a simultaneous attack on the Post of Castile and on St Michael was to be expected. This would prevent him sending reinforcements to the latter, as he would have to conserve his men to defend the main fortress of Castile. Since he was so conscious of de Aguilar's abilities, La Valette treated his desertion most seriously, and made what arrangements he could for our defence so as to defeat the enemy's plan. Accordingly, he had Captain Claramonte hand over the Post of the Spur of St Michael to the crew of the galley *Capitana*. As his new post he took over all the area between Buoninsegna and Maldonado, taking with him for this purpose the crew of the galley *St Gabriel*. Despite the fact that the main wall of this part was totally razed, it had a counterfosse behind it, with casemates and a good trench system. At the same time, the knights and soldiers were withdrawn from all the posts that were in least danger, and were divided between the Posts of Castile and St Michael. He gave a further directive that, as soon as the alarm sounded, Commander de Guiral with his men and the Piliers of England and Germany with theirs, should rally in the square where the reliefs gathered. Furthermore, the Grand Master saw to it that there should always be fires burning at the posts so as to keep the cauldrons of pitch on the boil, as well as to ignite the hoops which I have earlier described. The posts in greatest danger were to be kept well supplied with bags of gunpowder, sulphur, incendiaries, pikes, and the incendiary trumps. All were to be kept under a strong guard. These positions were also to be furnished with planks studded with large nails, and these were to be sited wherever the enemy was most likely to jump into the fortifications. La Valette also gave orders that whenever attacks started, supplies of powder for the arquebuses, cannon balls, and plenty of lighted ropes' ends were to be constantly supplied to the threatened positions. These also were to be kept under careful supervision and a strong guard.

The Grand Master gave instructions that as soon as the *Angelus* sounded in the morning, all the fires were to be immediately lit, the pitch-hoops made ready, and the cauldrons brought to the boil. In short, everything was to be brought to the highest degree of readiness for it was certain that we must soon undergo an all-out attack. We, for our part, carried out all his orders most diligently and we often stood to our stations, even though the enemy made no move.

XI

THE BRAVERY OF THE GRAND
MASTER. OUR CAVALRY ATTACK
THE TURKISH BASE CAMP

Tuesday, 7 August. It was an hour before daybreak when we saw that all the enemy on Corradino had begun to move down towards St Michael. Men from the fleet also embarked at Marsamuscetto and were transported to Mount Salvador, and these movements were a clear sign that we might expect a general assault during the day, as indeed it turned out. For, as soon as it was light, they attacked St Michael and the Post of Castile *en masse*, with such an uproar and blare of military music, that we would have marvelled if we had not grown familiar with it on other occasions.

Eight thousand Turks attacked St Michael on this day, and four thousand the Post of Castile. They all came in a rush together, according to plan, and as we had anticipated. But as soon as they left their trenches, we were ready for them – the incendiary hoops blazing, the pitch boiling, and everything primed for our defence. The result was that when they began to scale the battlements, they were received like men who were well-expected. The attacks made on this day were violent, and fought out on both sides with much bloodshed and cruelty. The main attack fell, just as we had expected it would, on the Post of Marshal Robles, and on Bormla where Bernardo de Cabrera was in command. These were the weakest parts of the defences, and seemed therefore the easiest to capture. It was here that the main battle took place, the enemy pouring in the mass of their troops, and it was here also that the incendiaries wrought the greatest havoc among them, as well as the fire from the two traverses which, sited opposite one another, brought a cross-fire to bear upon the attacking enemy. The Turkish artillery did not fire during the assault, so as to avoid killing their own men advancing in close formation over open ground. On this day, as on all others, we fought from our positions behind cover, having learnt from bitter experience in the past.

The attack on the Post of Castile was no less serious than that on

St Michael. There was a moment during the battle around Castile, when a Knight of the Order, a man of some importance, ran up to the Grand Master (who was standing in the square with the relief force, waiting to go wherever he might be required), and cried: 'My Lord, come to the aid of Castile! The Turks are breaking in!' The Grand Master, without showing a trace of emotion, replied:

'Come, my knights, let us all go and die there! This is the day!'

With this, he took his helmet from one page and his pike from the other, and with exemplary courage led the way to Castile, followed by all the reserves. As soon as he reached the gate that led to the place of danger, the Bailiff of the Eagle, La Motta, Captain Romegas, and other notables tried to prevent him from going to the post of danger. But, to their dismay, he insisted on going forward, and even tried to climb up the spur of the cavalier of Castile, where the enemy were already established. Here they did manage to hold him back, for it was completely open to the Turkish fire from both Salvador and Kalkara, and he went instead to the battery of Claramonte, pike in hand, as if he were no more than a common soldier. Then, looking up and seeing the spur of Buoninsegna's post thick with Turks, he seized an arquebus from a soldier and aiming at the enemy, opened fire, calling out at the same time: 'This way, boys, this way!'

All our men in this battery immediately aimed up at the enemy and opened a rapid fire. At the same time, those above began hurling incendiaries and rocks with such good effect that the Turks were forced to retire with heavy losses.

When the principal knights saw that the danger was over, they persuaded the Grand Master to retire from where he stood, surrounded as he was by more than twenty dead. Then, like the great soldier he was – who knew that, after God, our salvation depended upon his life – he consented to withdraw. But he had no intention of resting, for he would go no further than the gate of the inner defences, and there he stayed. Although it always grieved him to see our dead, he pointed out that none of them had died in vain, and praised the dead so as to put courage into the living. It was during this action that La Valette was wounded in the leg, yet all the same he did not relax from going the rounds, even though his leg was in bandages.

During this attack the Royal Standard of the Sultan Suleiman was seen above the walls of Castile at the Post of Buoninsegna. It had a white horse's tail and many tassels attached to it. Seeing it, we hurled hooked lines to try and get hold of it, and at last we managed to do so. As a result of our pulling one way, and the Turks pulling the other, the ball on top of the shaft fell off, which enabled them to save the sultan's standard, but not before we had burned many of its silk and gold tassels with incendiaries.

The attacks lasted for nine hours, from daybreak until just after noon. The Turks were relieved more than a dozen times by fresh troops, while we refreshed ourselves with well-watered wine and a few mouthfuls of bread. The Grand Master in his foresight, realizing that, unlike the enemy, we could have no relief because we were so few, saw to it that we always had some refreshment like this. He had given orders that whenever we were under attack plenty of bottles of watered wine, as well as bread, should be available at all the posts which were engaged. A further instance of his foresight were the barrels of salt water, which were kept in great numbers at all the posts, to provide relief for those who had been burned. Had it not been for the many wise precautions made by the Grand Master, no men could have stood up to the persistent onslaughts.

Victory was ours this day, but through Divine Help rather than through human endeavour. The enemy had intended that this should be their last assault and, in order to make sure, they had left not a single man in their camp, nor even anyone who could fight in the fleet. As for us, in spite of all the help and guidance given us by the Grand Master, there was not a man who could stand upright from fatigue or wounds. We lost a great many dead, yet our Lord God came to our help in the following way.

After these attacks had been going on for nine hours it would seem that Our Lord inspired the cavalry who were in Mdina. They were going out in their usual way and, not seeing a single Turk anywhere in the island, they pressed on as far as the Marsa. It was here that they realized the great danger to which the Order was exposed. Not knowing how else they could help us – for they were only a hundred horse and about the same number of infantry – they decided to make an attack on the sick and the other noncombatants quartered there. They killed all whom they found, shouting as they did so: 'Victory and Relief!' Now some Turks from the fleet who were stationed on the promontory of St Elmo, were the first to see what was happening in the Marsa, and forming up into a squadron, they set off in that direction. When the Turks who were attacking the Posts of Castile and St Michael, noticed that this squadron moved forward no more than a hundred paces before turning and fleeing back towards the fleet, they stopped fighting and gave up their attack. Just then the pasha in charge of the army [Mustapha] was

K

told that all those who had been left behind in the Marsa were dead, and the tents destroyed.

When this news reached the trenches, the rumour got around that a strong relief had arrived to help us, and that if they did not retreat hastily they would all be slaughtered. This story, false though it was, had such an effect that the Turks all withdrew from their trenches, without waiting for any orders from the pasha or from their officers. The troops facing the Post of Castile were the first to move. As they came out of the ditch, they were fired upon by our arquebusiers at the Post of Auvergne, and many were killed. The enemy attacking St Michael, seeing what was happening on the promontory of St Elmo, did not know what to do. Very soon their wounded came pouring in, saying that our forces were a thousand men. At this point the enemy did not wait, but fled from their trenches, and none of their officers could stop them.

We were completely astounded by this sudden retreat, for we had no idea what had happened. We thought perhaps that it might be due to some disagreement between the two pashas, or some other trouble (things that quite often happen in war), or even that some renegades had made off with part of their fleet. It did occur to us that perhaps some relief force of our own had landed and was hard on the enemy's heels, but it wasn't long before we learned the truth from the Sicilians who, from their post, had been the first to see our cavalry fighting in the Marsa with sword in hand. They at once told the Grand Master, who sent a scout to the top of the clock tower to find out the truth of the matter.

The Sicilians now began to shout: 'Victory, victory! Relief, relief!' The word was passed on from post to post, striking fear into the hearts of the Turks while it put new heart into us. While no Turk could be seen anywhere in their trenches, there was not a single Christian who did not mount upon the rampart. Not understanding what had happened, Mustapha Pasha formed his men up and marched them in order on Santa Margarita, where he could take advantage of a secure position and of the artillery sited there. As soon as he reached it, he halted, waiting to find out what had really taken place. It was not long before the Turks realized that a handful of men had snatched victory from their grasp, putting them to shameful flight.

The Turks now began to advance again, with their banners unfurled, in the direction of our cavalry. Warned in advance by their sentries, every horseman took a foot-soldier up behind him and, without losing a single man and having inflicted many casualties on the enemy, they retired back into Mdina. It is impossible to describe how humiliated the pashas, and indeed all their army, felt when they saw how small a force had caused them such grievous harm and in-stilled such fear into their hearts. Mustapha was the angriest of all and, in his fury, he turned on Piali. 'If you', he said, 'had marched on the Marsa after you had formed up your men, this panic would never have occurred. Even if you had not advanced, you should never have retreated in such haste and disorder.'

Piali replied that he had been told that a great Christian relief force had landed. If such were the case, he felt it was his duty to save the fleet. 'The sultan', he said, 'thinks much more of the fleet than he does of an army like this one.' With this reply he walked off.

Over two thousand men must have been killed this day in the attack on St Michael, if one is to judge by the haste with which the enemy retrieved their dead. Their wounded, as we learned later, were double that number. Over two hundred of their most dis-tinguished men were killed in the attack on Castile, among them Ochali the Greek.* Our total losses were sixty dead, but we had a great many more wounded.

Even the knights who were not actually engaged in the fighting played an important part. On La Valette's orders they kept guard over the other positions – some of which were very lightly defended – as most of the knights and troops had gone to reinforce those that were threatened. I must not omit to mention the courage shown throughout the siege by the very young knights of the Order. They fought in the most dangerous positions, readily taking the place of the fallen, and showed as much courage and spirit as if they had been veterans. The innumerable and horrible deaths that they wit-nessed daily did not deter them. Since I do not know all their names, I shall not mention any of them for I have no wish to appear partial – and this I certainly am not.

No sooner had all the Turks retired from St Michael, than Mar-shal Robles fell on his knees before us all, giving thanks to God for the great victory He had granted us. He sent a message to the Grand Master, asking him to have a *Te Deum* sung in the Church of St Lawrence, for we had been blessed with one of the greatest victories that Christians had ever gained. When the bearer of the message arrived, he found that there was no point in delivering it, for the

* This was Ochali Fartas, one of the most notorious pirates in the Aegean and the Levant.

Grand Master was already giving thanks – as he always did when the Turks had been beaten off – and the *Te Deum* asked for by Robles was already being solemnly celebrated. After it was over, there was a procession and, even if it was not as formal as those which the Order is accustomed to make, the tears of many men and women nevertheless gave it the tribute of their devotion.

There were inevitably some who, affecting a great solicitude for the safety of the Grand Master, advised him to retire within St Angelo, but they did so really because they saw how wide the breaches in the walls were and believed that we could not resist any longer. They suggested that he should take with him the best part of the Order, and wait there in greater security until the relief arrived. This suggestion became known to the troops, and each one of us spoke his mind as to what he thought of such advisers. But the Grand Master, when he became acquainted with it – he who was always ready to be the first to die for his Order – had all the relics and everything of great value taken into St Angelo. But, so that there should be no doubt of his intentions, he had the bridge removed, making it clear to the whole world that there would be no retreat, and that we should either die in Birgu or successfully defend it.

Now before the enemy made this last attack they had already driven some well-covered trenches right up to the mouth of the ditch of Castile. This point was defended by the casemate of Auvergne with eight gun positions, four above, and the other four in the ditch itself. However, because there was little room, this casemate could not mount large guns. Seeing what casualties they suffered whenever they attacked Castile, or indeed when they retired from it, and realizing that their guns could not give them covering fire or put the casemate out of action, the Turks, when they reached the entrance to this ditch, decided to dig a trench there. This trench would allow them to go in and out, and would be strong enough to give them protection against the fire from the casemate. Keeping to the right of the guns of the spur of the cavalier, where it was under fire from Kalkara, they managed to dig the trench right up to the outer defence of the counterfosse, and there was nothing that we could do to stop them, although we were continually hurling rocks and incendiaries from our parapet.

Having reached the wall, the Turks cut an opening in it and began to throw earth and brushwood into the ditch. As soon as the level was up to that of the opening, they pushed their trench further out into the ditch. They managed to do all this even though they were under fire from a small cannon that Captain Romegas had mounted at this point, and where he himself spent the whole day laying and firing it, causing great losses among the enemy. In order to restrain the recoil of this cannon, since there was very little room, Romegas had a great heap of rope placed behind it to act as a shock-absorber.

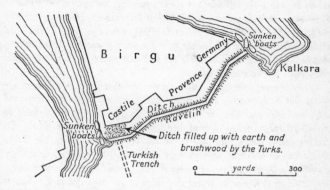

After three-quarters of their trench had been completed, the enemy were safe, and in a short time they were able to finish it. While they were engaged on this operation, the Grand Master was told how impossible it was to stop them and that, when the trench was completed, it would prove a grave menace. So he had a tunnel dug from inside the walls to the right of this trench at the spur of the cavalier. The idea was that from here we could either attack any men who got into the ditch, or could use the tunnel for going out to raid their trench. But when our tunnel was finished, we discovered that the two guns on Kalkara, the ones which had bombarded the traverses at the Post of Don Rodrigo Maldonado, commanded the exit. Accordingly we left it, and did not open it through the wall, thinking that it might serve on some other occasion. Meanwhile we constructed a number of other ingenious defences within the walls.

The attack by the cavalry from Mdina on the Turkish base camp, distasteful though the slaughter of wounded and unarmed men must be to the modern reader, undoubtedly saved the day. As ever throughout the siege, one sees that it was Admiral Piali's incessant preoccupation with the safety of his fleet that bedevilled the whole Turkish enterprise. A further important point which must be noted about Balbi's entry for this day is La Valette's refusal to retreat

into Fort St Angelo with a chosen handful of the Order. St Angelo was undoubtedly the strongest of all the defences and, indeed, the only fort in Malta
at that time which approached the strength of the fortifications that the knights
had formerly built in Rhodes. While the two pashas made innumerable mis-
takes in the conduct of the campaign, La Valette would seem to have been
almost faultless in his strategy throughout. His insistence that St Elmo
should be held to the last man and the last moment, had enabled the defenders
of the two main peninsulas to complete their preparations. His construction of
the bridge of boats between the peninsula of Birgu and that of St Michael had
enabled reliefs to be rushed quickly from one point to another. His insistence
that both peninsulas be defended to the last man forced the Turks to divide
their troops and their artillery.

Commentators other than Balbi have recorded that at one time it was suggested that St Michael be abandoned, and everyone withdrawn into Birgu and
St Angelo. It was then, as we learn here, suggested that Birgu itself be
abandoned and a selected party of defenders left to await relief in St Angelo.
Such a course would have been disastrous. Within a day or so, the Turks
would have been able to concentrate the entire fire of their formidable artillery
on St Angelo, which – strong though it was – would never have been able to
withstand it. It is also on record that when it was suggested to La Valette
that he abandon Birgu he said that he would never leave the faithful Maltese
men and women to the mercy of the Turk, and that it would be better no one
was left alive than that anyone should be saved under such disgraceful conditions. The bridge which La Valette ordered to be destroyed, connected St
Angelo with Birgu across a sea-water moat. This no longer exists. The
fortress and the town were linked in the nineteenth century, although there is a
small boat-harbour in the place where the ditch was in La Valette's time.

XII

FURTHER ATTACKS ARE MADE ON ST MICHAEL AND CASTILE BUT NEWS IS RECEIVED THAT A RELIEF FORCE IS ON ITS WAY

Wednesday, 8 August. Hardly any Turks were to be seen in their trenches. This, as we found out later, was because they had marched on Mdina to try and avenge themselves for the losses they had sustained. They wanted, if possible, to lure the cavalry outside the city. With this in mind, they prepared three ambushes: one by the Grand Master's Wood; the other by the village of Zebbug; and the third by San Domingo. A great number of arquebusiers moved on to the plain in front of the old city, and began to carry off the cattle grazing there. As soon as our men saw this, they sallied out to engage the enemy, who retreated in order to lure our troops away from Mdina and into one of the ambushes. Our men made contact with the Turks, recovered the cattle, and were about to return to the city,

when they caught sight of the enemy who had been lying in ambush dashing across to cut them off. Captain Anastasio and Captain Lugny, as soon as they realized what the Turks were up to, left the cattle safe where they were under cover of our artillery fire, and marched on the enemy. Charging the Turks, they killed over fifty of them and routed the rest, but lost twelve of their own men and thirty horses. It was for this reason that we saw few Turks in the trenches this day, although there was some artillery fire, mostly directed at the houses.

It was at this time that Captain Andreas de Salazar had been sent down by Don Garcia to spy out the Turkish camp.* He was an experienced old soldier, and his orders were to make a report when he returned. Taking advantage of the opportunity to reconnoitre the area by St Leonard and the Belvedere, Salazar saw that there was every chance of a small force putting the Turks to flight, and he made his report accordingly.

Salazar, Lugny, Vincenzo Anastasi, and his lieutenant Vincenzo Ventura, all good knights and experienced soldiers, took part in the action against the three Turkish attempts at ambush. Ventura and the men with him were pursued by the largest party of Turks but he, being a quick-witted man, leapt from his horse. His soldiers did the same, and in the darkness and over the uneven ground they managed to escape and get back to Mdina – where they had already been given up as lost. In this engagement our men also met lance-to-lance with Piali, who had himself gone out with the Turkish troops.

Thursday, 9 August. We were bombarded until noon, when a feint was made against St Michael and Castile, but the enemy retired without having had any success. Being now in control of the entrance to the ditch of Castile, the Turks began to throw a vast quantity of stones into it so as to get rid of the water and to make it possible to cross. At the same time they began digging another trench by the sea-shore, just as they had done near St Michael, and drove it right up to the Post of Don Rodrigo Maldonado. They also constructed a covered passage near St Michael, in front of the Post of Marshal Robles. This was quickly finished, and it led up to the place where the large barrels had stood.† Having pushed this covered passage near to the barrels, they then made a shelter capable of holding a hundred men, their intention being to take this position by assault at some time when our men were occupied in fighting elsewhere. To prevent this happening, Marshal Robles, on the advice of Mathias de Rivera, had a gun platform constructed inside the wall. It was semi-circular in shape, with a covered embrasure in front. Here he had a light quick-firing gun mounted, which was kept

---

* De Salazar was sent down by boat from Sicily, landed in the north of Malta, and thus made his way to Mdina. It was largely due to his reporting that the Turkish morale had collapsed that Don Garcia decided at last to take some action.

† The barrels, as we learned earlier, had been destroyed but, as they had been full of earth, it must be presumed that there was still a large mound at this point.

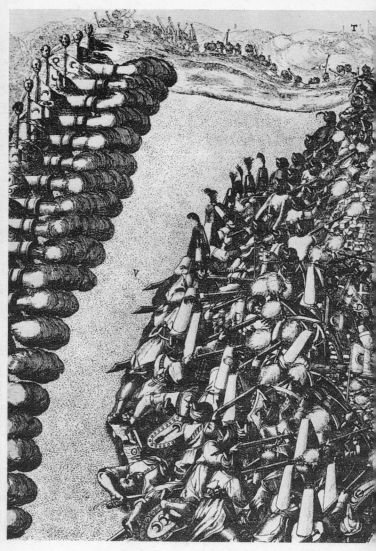

THE ASSAULT ON THE POST OF CASTILE

a. Grand Master La Valette: b. His major-domo Luis Villa: c. Cannon commanded by
Romegas: d. The place where our artillery commander was killed: e. The position from
which our men caused many Turkish casualties: f. The Post of Genoa: g. The Post of
Germany: h. Santa Margarita: i. The Belvedere: k. The place where the Turks broke in:

l. A soldier crying out 'Victory!': m. A Turk who killed numbers of our men: n. A Turkish trench: o. Ochiali the Corsair: p. A battery of 16 cannon, 2 basilisks, and 2 mortars: q. The heads of knights displayed on poles: r. Buoninsegna's Post: s. A Turkish entrenchment: t. Mount Calcara: v. Calcara Creek: x. A Turkish flag on the parapet.

loaded with chain-shot in a constant state of readiness. A light was also kept burning so that fire could be opened at any given moment.

Friday, 10 August. There was very little bombardment during the morning, but at the hour of the midday meal over a thousand Turks advanced in front of St Michael. The action can be called a genuine attack since fighting went on for two hours and they must have lost over a hundred men. The same afternoon they made another similar attack and lost a great deal more for, having continued the assault for a whole hour in a most determined manner, they were forced to retire yet again with heavy casualties. The fact remains that, in this engagement, it was never necessary for St Michael to call on reinforcements from Birgu.

The object of these attacks was not so much St Michael itself. The Turks hoped that we would send over a strong reinforcement from Birgu – when they would have at once made a major assault on the Post of Castile. Their plan did not succeed.

Saturday, 11 August. The enemy bombardment kept up all night, and continued right through the day. It was on this night that Marshal Robles – wanting to see for himself what effect the bombardment was having, as well as to have a look at the covered way which the Turks had made in front of his post – went out on top of the battlements of St Michael. By an unhappy accident he was not wearing his bullet-proof helmet – God knows, never did he need it more. As he was gazing down from the wall, an arquebusier in the enemy trenches took aim at him. He was hit in the head, and fell to the ground without a word. He lay in great pain and did not die until the following morning, regretted by every one of us. Not one of his soldiers, brave men though they were, would go to view his body. They did indeed love him more than their own lives, but they did not want to display their sorrow – for who could hold back tears for a man such as he? This was no time to weep or show any weakness and, said they, God would surely receive his soul. Furthermore, though Marshal Robles was dead, there were many more like him still left alive.

The marshal's body was laid to rest in the Church of St Lawrence in a coffin covered with black velvet and with a coloured cross upon it. The Grand Master said that if, with God's mercy, we should survive the siege, he would see that the marshal's body was sent back in honour to his relatives. Soon after the death of Marshal Robles, Muñatones (who had been wounded in Birgu) also died. The Grand Master appointed Chiaparro, Sergeant of the Company, in his place. At the same time, the Bailiff of the Eagle took over Marshal Robles' Post, and Don Pedro de Mendoza, a senior knight of Castile, and a brave and notable soldier, was made Captain of the Reserves.

Sunday, 12 August. We were expecting an assault, but learned that this had been postponed since a mine that the Turks were preparing under the Post of Castile was not quite ready. Having discovered this mine, we drove a counter mine against it, and a Spanish soldier called Matamoros killed four Turks in it with his arquebus.* On the following day, however, he was himself killed by the enemy.

Monday, 13 August. Only St Michael and its houses were bombarded, the Turks meantime trying to get to the top of the ruined cavalier by hacking away with picks and shovels. Seeing this, we poured every kind of incendiary upon them. But it was to no avail, for we were unable to look over our ramparts and take aim since their trenches – as I have explained – were so strongly manned. The Grand Master, with his usual foresight, had a twenty-foot-thick inner wall constructed in the cavalier. It ran so far back that our mine lay outside of it. On this day Juan de Funes was killed in Castile by artillery fire.

Wednesday, 15 August. The Turks advanced to the point of our cavalier, but could go no further because of our inner wall which was about the height of a man. At the Post of Castile, there was nothing between us and the enemy but this barrier. The Turks, from their position on the cavalier, set out to kill anyone entering this position, as well as anyone in the Post of Claramonte, between the positions commanded by Buoninsegna and Maldonado. With this in mind, the Turks constructed a fortification capable of holding twenty men. At the same time they made a trench right up to the Post of Maldonado. This had a number of loopholes in it for arquebus fire and from it, unless we found some counter measure, they would be able to shoot us down at leisure. The Grand Master, seeing what their intention was, had some light swivel-guns mounted at the entrance to our inner defence-work with which to knock down the Turkish entrenchment on top of the cavalier, but unfortunately they were too light to have much effect against so strong a position. Until we could find some remedy, La Valette gave orders for a number of traverses of thick stone to be built at the Post of Claramonte, high enough to give good cover. At the same time he had an opening cut in our inner defence-wall, and a gun emplace-

* 'Matamoros' was probably a nickname. It means 'kill Moors'.

ment constructed there. When it was completed a heavy cannon was brought into place to bombard the Turkish entrenchment on the cavalier. Its fire wrought havoc among the enemy, as we could tell by their efforts to put it out of action with gunfire from Kalkara (the same guns which had been bombarding the traverses of the Post of Maldonado). By the Grace of God they were unsuccessful, although they did hit it on one occasion, killing the Commander of the Artillery who was sitting astride the gun.

During the day the Bailiff of the Eagle, who had taken Marshal Robles' place at St Michael, was wounded by an arquebus shot, and died ten days later. He was now succeeded as Marshal by a French Knight of the Grand Cross and a notable soldier, who stayed in command at this post until the very end.

Although it was quite clear to us that the Turks on the cavalier of Buoninsegna were suffering heavy losses from our cannon, they refused to abandon the position and so show that their morale had been sapped. All they did was to withdraw a little, until they were safely protected from our inner defences, which we ourselves would damage if we opened fire on them. Observing the situation, the Grand Master, and the commanders in charge of these posts, ordered us to make a sortie by night, to try and drive the enemy from their position. Our party was getting ready to go out, when it was discovered that one of the men who had been detailed was not with us. He was a Spanish soldier of fortune, a friend of Claramonte and a man of great courage. It was not his fault that he was not there, for he had not been told the time that we were to leave. Grand Master La Valette himself was present to see the expedition set off. Thinking it time that they started, he asked the reason for the delay, and was informed that they were waiting for a Spanish soldier. Now Mendoza, another Spanish soldier in the company of Claramonte, a man who had previously served under Don Francisco de Sanoguera, was standing near by. Hearing that a Spanish soldier was missing, and knowing who it was, he immediately said: 'I am here.' By joining the small band of five men on this raiding party, Mendoza saved the honour of his friend – a noble action, which is why I have recorded it.

The party sallied forth, led by a Maltese, an extremely brave and fine man. He was followed by Mendoza, and then the others. So determined was their attack, and so great their courage, that the Turks on the cavalier of Buoninsegna were forced to retreat with considerable losses. There followed considerable activity in the Turkish camp. Seeing they could not recapture the position and could not, furthermore, open fire for fear of hitting their own men, they managed to fix a lantern to a lance. This they set up to the right of the spur and used it as an aiming mark. As soon as our men saw this they started to hurl incendiaries and shoot at it, keeping this up until it was smashed. Round about dawn our six men came back, bringing with them all the belongings that the Turks had left behind. They found that they could not stay in the place they had captured because it was open to the enemy's artillery fire. However, before coming back within our lines, they destroyed the position.

Thursday, 16 August. The enemy carried out a general bombardment, very heavy fire being directed on us from all quarters. At the same time, the Turks improved their own situation by reinforcing their trenches, as well as by sapping under our defences. To protect themselves against the rocks and incendiaries which we hurled down upon them, they used shields of ox-hides and goatskins.

Thursday, 16 August to Monday, 20 August. Throughout this period the Turks kept up their bombardment, but achieved no more than before, because our defences were as flattened as they could ever be. At the Post of Castile nothing stood between us and the Turks save the inner defence (ten or twelve feet thick), and at St Michael only the remains of the large barrels. Christian renegades in the Turkish ranks, moved by our plight, called across to our men from their trenches, taking pity on us as they had many times done before. The Turks doubtless thought that they were heaping insults upon us. In fact they were helping us for, although their words were veiled, we were able to read their underlying meaning. For instance they shouted to us: 'You dogs, hold out! You haven't got many oxen to kill. There are only sheep left and they are weak ones, weak ones! There is no more flour, and with the next assault you will be free!' What they intended us to understand by this was, that they had no good troops left, nor powder for the guns, but that all the same we must expect one more assault. The Grand Master had other good reasons for expecting them to try another general assault. Our defences were ruined, and winter was not far off – when their fleet would no longer be able to stay at sea. What was more, they had lost vast numbers of men, and expended so much ammunition (for they were now using up the ammunition which belonged to the fleet) that it was inevitable they should make one last and final attempt.

The Grand Master showed himself in every way to be not only a great leader, but a good and practical soldier. There was no type of work from which he spared himself, whether physical or mental, in keeping us on our toes and ready for every emergency. He would sleep in the most exposed positions, and made night rounds constantly, even though the knights in charge begged him not to risk his life but to take care of himself.

Meanwhile the pashas were continually exhorting the few Janissaries and Spahis who were left, to make another assault. But they replied that they had no desire to, and that they were astounded the pashas should wish, out of sheer obstinacy, to lose the few men that remained – and with them the honour of the sultan. If the pashas were prepared to risk their own lives, they would indeed follow them in as many attacks as they wanted. When Mustapha Pasha heard this he could not restrain himself and called them cowards, saying that they were not worthy of their title: 'Sons of the Sultan'. A man in his position, he said, was not called upon to risk his life, but he was willing to be first in the attack and show that he could face danger as well as any other man. The Janissaries then replied that, whenever he chose to do so, they would follow him.

Monday, 20 August. It was just dawn when the enemy made a concerted attack on St Michael and Castile. They advanced with their usual shouts and clamour of musical instruments. Mustapha Pasha himself was in their front rank and, though he was a man of sixty, he showed himself to be full of courage. An ingenious stratagem he contrived was to have the camp servants dressed in the uniforms of those Janissaries and Spahis who had been killed. His hope was that this would inspire them with courage. He had even promised them that, if they fought well, he would have them made Janissaries. When Mustapha Pasha came into the section where the fire from our traverses was falling, a shot from Bormla knocked his turban from his head and stunned him. A little while later, he crawled on all fours to take refuge in the ditch of St Michael, where he stayed until it was dark.

This attack lasted all of five hours, the enemy being relieved many times by waves of fresh troops, while we refreshed ourselves as well as we could in our usual way. The assault this morning was one of the most violent of the whole siege, the Turkish arquebus fire and bombardment doing an immense amount of damage. While this was going on, the Grand Master was once again alarmed by a report from the Post of Castile. He was told, as he was standing in the square, that the enemy were already inside the Post. With his customary calm courage, he rushed to the threatened position, sword in hand. His presence inspired the defenders, and he stayed there at the point of danger until the enemy retired.

Four attacks were made during the day, two on St Michael and two on Castile. The morning attack lasted five hours and the afternoon attack three hours. The intention was to wear us down by continuous assault. Commander Buoninsegna, that good soldier and knight, was wounded by an incendiary, and was relieved by Don Juan de Pereyra. His post was the one in which Commander Cencio Guasconi had been wounded by musket fire while making a reconnaissance over the wall to see what the enemy were doing.

Grand Master La Valette was greatly concerned about the fate of St Michael, the worst thing being that he could not send any reliefs since the other troops were fully engaged at the Post of Castile. Knowing how anxious he must be, the new marshal, as soon as the Turks had withdrawn, sent forty men under Giulio Crudeli, Martello's ensign, to give assistance to Castile. He also sent a message to the Grand Master not to worry about St Michael since it was stronger than ever. The Marshal added that if he needed more men, he would send them to him. Only God knows how much this message of hope encouraged La Valette.

The Turkish losses during the day's attack were over two hundred, not counting their wounded, while our own losses were very few. Among our dead was Master Marco, La Valette's tailor, a Maltese born and bred, who on this day as on all others fought like a good Christian and a gallant soldier. After fighting like a veritable Hector, he was burned to death by incendiaries at the Post of Commander Maldonado. We had very few wounded during the day's action. On this occasion many of the convalescents, although not completely recovered, lent a hand at the defences when the Turks attacked. They did whatever they were able, like brave men, for they preferred to die in battle rather than be cruelly slaughtered in the hospital – as they would have been if the Turks, to our great anguish, had managed to take Birgu.

Tuesday, 21 August. There was another general assault during the morning, every bit as fierce as on the day before. After four hours' fighting, both at Castile and St Michael, the enemy retired with heavy losses. Castile was in a most desperate plight, for there were so few defenders left and every day these were being whittled away. The worst moment during the attack on Castile occurred at the peak of the battle when one of our men and a Turk, both carrying flame-throwing guns, came face to face. Now the Turk had a trump which was loaded with bullets as big as doves' eggs, and when these two fired their weapons the result could not have been more disastrous. The bullets from the Turk's trump killed a number of our men, while at the same time the flame from it set fire to all our fire-grenades and other incendiary weapons, causing us terrible losses. However, by the Grace of God, the flame from our soldier's weapon touched off the sacks of gunpowder belonging to the enemy, and burned a great many of them to death. If it had not been for this we would have been in a position of utmost peril, for the enemy were already established on the Post of Maldonado which had very few defenders left. It was only just in time that the Grand Master arrived, together with the few men who were all that were left to him of the reserves; but these were enough to force the Turks to retire. It was during this attack that Don Rodrigo de Maldonado was wounded, Sagra being appointed to relieve him.

As well as making these repeated attacks, the enemy now started building a kind of bastion with sacks of wool and cotton at the foot of the battery of Robles. (The post kept his name, even though he was dead.) It seemed that what the Turks intended to do, was to build this bastion high enough so as to dominate our defences and spread havoc among us when next they came to the attack.

Friday, 24 August. During the second watch of the night, our troops sallied out from the Posts of Robles and Bormla into the enemy's trenches. So sudden and unexpected was their attack that the Turks fled before them, and they managed to break down the new bastion. They brought back with them many sacks of wool, shovels, picks, and other tools. Everything else they set on fire.

For the next forty-eight hours the enemy continued to make both real and feigned assaults, in which, Thank Heaven, they had no success. Already there were signs of approaching winter, for the north wind started to blow and there was some heavy rain. In view of this, the Grand Master had the soldiers issued with coverings made of woven grass, to give them some protection while they were carrying out their duties. It was also clear to La Valette that the enemy must certainly take advantage of the rain to make an attack on us, since it would afford them some protection against our incendiaries and arquebus fire. To remedy this, he had the posts which were in the greatest danger equipped with a large number of cross-bows that we had in store. In this way he dashed the enemy's hopes, for they attacked us a number of times while it was raining, but soon found out that it was we who had the advantage, for they could not use their bows, while our cross-bows were so powerful that a bolt from one of them could pierce a shield, and even the man behind it.

During the afternoon we killed a Turk in front of the Post of Don Bernardo de Cabrera. The enemy were afraid to try and recover his body because of the arquebusiers stationed there. In order to shame them, Don Bernardo sallied out with Don Juan Mascon and some Maltese soldiers, and – to the humiliation of the Turks – cut off the dead man's head and stuck it upon a post. Yet still the enemy persisted by day and night, so determined were they to bring the siege to a successful conclusion in one way or another. Seeing that the bastion which they had built with sacks of wool had been destroyed, they adopted another siege weapon, which was called a *testudo* by the ancients, and which is known today as a *manta*.* It was similar to those which the Emperor Charles V used at Terruana and Artois. They got it ready at the entrance to the covered way which I have described, intending to approach under its protection as far as 'the Barrels'. They would then break in at that point during the next assault. However, as soon as it was spotted, Matias de Ribera, a soldier of fortune, had a masked gun-port made ready for use when the time came.

Monday, 27 August. It was immediately clear that the enemy were going to attack, for in the morning we could see their men crossing from Santaren in the direction of Castile, and from the Marsa to the

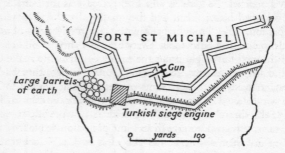

trenches opposite St Michael. When the time was ripe they began to move the *manta* towards 'the Barrels', and we let them get so near that we could not miss them. At a given moment, the gun [in the masked embrasure] was fired, and the *manta* was blown to pieces, as well as

---

* The *testudo* or 'tortoise' was an arrangement of overlapping shields, or reinforced leather hides, which gave protection to the men working underneath it.

about forty Turks who were behind it. With the loss of their siege engine, and of the men manning it, they gave up the attack.

During the night our troops sallied out from Castile in the direction of the Turkish trenches, but the enemy fled before an engagement could take place. Having destroyed part of their trenches, our men came back bringing with them many of the ox-hides the Turks had been using to protect themselves against our stones, as well as many shovels, picks, and biscuits. In the course of the same night we also recaptured the spur of the cavalier. But, as it was exposed to their artillery fire, we could not hold it during the day. The Turks came back at dawn, and there was a steady exchange of hand grenades and rocks between them and us for the rest of the day. Seeing that there was no other way of dislodging the Turks from the spur of the cavalier, the Grand Master gave instructions for a mine to be made, designed so that when it was exploded it would not damage our defences. As soon as it was ready, a time was chosen when the spur was occupied by Turks. It was then blown up, taking over forty of them with it.

Tuesday, 28 August. Throughout the day and night there was a heavy bombardment of the houses and the fortifications. However, in spite of this, we knew that they had embarked a great number of their guns, for each night we could hear them being withdrawn – even though it was done very stealthily, and with none of the triumphant shouts with which they had been brought up. It was now that the Grand Master asked Lorenzo Puche, a soldier from Claramonte's company, if he were willing to go down into the enemy trenches and find out if they were manned – for there seemed to be no one in them. He answered bravely that he was quite willing to go. However, while he was getting ready, he was hit by an arquebus shot which dented his helmet and knocked him to the ground. This was witnessed by the Grand Master and, when Puche picked himself up and asked permission to carry on, he refused to allow him to venture out. It was now arranged that Don Bernardo de Cabrera and Don Juan Mascon should go out that night with some soldiers, by way of the Post of Provence into the trenches at Bormla. It was not until they had left St Michael and gone to Birgu, that the attempt was called off. Their aim had been to try and capture a Turk in the trenches near the shore by the Post of Aragon.

Wednesday, 29 August. The Turks attacked again in a mass assault, but they had to be driven to it by their officers with swords and sticks. Although we already held them in contempt, we did not forget to be on our guard. It was during the heaviest fighting of the day that, by God's Grace, a rainstorm forced them to retreat. They had achieved nothing, and had lost many men.

Thursday, 30 August. There was another attack on St Michael after midday. It lasted until nightfall, when the enemy withdrew having lost over a hundred men. We had one soldier killed, and three wounded.

Friday, 31 August. We were all ready for another attack, but the Turks made no move – for, as we realized, they were just as exhausted as we were ourselves. It was during this night that a Maltese, who had been captured at the beginning of the siege, escaped from their galleys and managed to reach Birgu. Speaking to the Grand Master publicly in the square, he said that the Turkish losses were very heavy (greater even than we had believed), and that the spirit had gone out of them. He said also that many of their labourers were dying of hunger and disease. The fleet did not leave because the guns had been taken from the ships, and sixty galleys were short of crews both sailors and oarsmen. He added that there was talk of reliefs being expected daily from Constantinople. He said also that a number of renegades had fled to Sicily, and for this reason a boom had been made out of spars and laid across the mouth of Marsamuscetto, to prevent any others sailing off with part of the fleet.

During the night a Maltese arrived from Mdina after a perilous journey, and said openly that Prince Giovanni Andrea Doria had arrived in person in one of his galleys and that he had taken stock of our situation. He had left behind a Spanish soldier called Martinez, who was to signal Don Garcia the news in the island, as soon as the latter appeared with his fleet. Don Garcia was on the verge of coming to our relief, but he was acting most circumspectly in view of the gravity of the situation.

Don Garcia had, in fact, already held a review of the relief force, on 22 August, when eight thousand men had been drawn up on the slopes above the harbour of Syracuse. The force was composed mainly of Spanish soldiers, although there were some professional soldiers from every country of Europe in its ranks. During the month of August, when the situation of the defenders had been critical, politics and dissensions had prevented the dispatch of the relief from Sicily. The party in favour of going to the relief of Malta had finally triumphed with the arrival of some two hundred knights, commanders, and Grand Crosses of the Order. They had complained about sitting idle in Messina while their brethren were dying in Malta, and Don Garcia had

daily to endure the sting of their disapproval. Vertot records that when Don
Garcia complained to one of them, Louis de Lastic, Grand Prior of Auvergne,
that he had not received from him the courtesy title of 'Excellency', which
was his due, the Grand Prior had replied: 'Sire, provided that we arrive in
Malta in time to save the Order I will give you what titles you please –
Excellency, Your Highness, or even, if you wish, Your Majesty'.

The relief force, unknown to La Valette, actually sailed on 25 August. Its
destination was the small islet of Linosa which lies sixty-five miles west of
Malta. There had been a previous arrangement between Don Garcia and La
Valette, that if, as was now the case, communications were impossible between Malta and Sicily, La Valette should send a boat with dispatches to
Linosa. La Valette had, in fact, already sent the boat to Linosa where, with
the latest dispatches, it was awaiting the arrival of Don Garcia. The reason
why the relief force did not reach Malta until 7 September, was that it fell
foul of a gale in the Malta–Sicily channel. As Balbi tells us later, it was dis-
persed and then took several days to re-form.

For obvious reasons Balbi does not indulge in any open criticism of Don
Garcia. After all, Balbi was only a common soldier, while Don Garcia was
the Viceroy of Sicily, a nobleman, and a friend of King Philip of Spain.
Furthermore Balbi's memoirs were, as we know, printed in Spain with the
licence of His Most Catholic Majesty. All the historians of the Order who
had access to the records and secret documents – which Balbi did not – are
unanimous in putting the blame for the late arrival of the relief on Don
Garcia's dilatoriness. There seems little doubt that, quite apart from any other
considerations, Don Garcia was frightened of a Turkish fleet, while he was at
sea with the relief force, leaving Malta and making a descent on undefended
Sicily.

XIII

ALTHOUGH THE TURKISH ATTACKS CONTINUE OUR RELIEF FORCE REACHES THE ISLAND

Saturday, 1 September. While the Turks were digging a mine they ran into ours at the Post of Castile, and took away two barrels of our gunpowder. They then used this to bombard us, as we knew from the thick black smoke, which was different from theirs. We were now so close to the enemy at every point, that we could have shaken hands with them. The Turks opposite St Michael gave Martello some local fruit, such as melons, and oranges. In exchange for these he gave them some white bread and cheese. When the Turks saw this, they were dumbfounded, for they had been convinced that we were extremely short of food. Indeed, they had threatened us with a long siege saying that they would reduce us by hunger if they could not do so by force.

At both these posts no man could show himself save with the greatest risk, for both sides were always on the alert, with their guns and slow-matches ready at all times to shoot down anyone the moment he was seen.* The Grand Master invented a method of firing at the enemy without risk to ourselves, by having two arquebuses lashed together on the top of a number of poles. The arquebuses were fixed aiming downwards, and we fired them by having the slow-match attached to a piece of string. It was inevitable that when we raised these above the defences and fired them, some of the Turks were hit. On a great number of occasions they tried to bring down these poles with hooks on lines, but we always managed to cut away their lines.

The cavalry now sallied out of Mdina and laid an ambush near the strait between Malta and Gozo. Some infantry hid in the rushes

---

* Before the discovery and general adoption of the hammer-and-flint lock for muskets, the slow-match was an essential part of the arquebusier's equipment. It was no more than a piece of rope or cord which had been impregnated with gunpowder and which, when once lit, would continue to smoulder for a long time. Larger slow-matches were always kept burning by the cannons. The effect of a heavy rainstorm was, as we have seen, to put nearly all the arquebuses out of action.

near a pool where the Turkish ships used to go to draw water. They were in hiding there one day, when a galleot came up and landed her men, whereupon our men attacked them, forced them to leave their water-barrels, and drove them in flight to their vessel. One of our cavalry men even launched his spear at a Turk on board the ship. If two other ships, which were on guard there, had not come to the rescue, the galleot would have been ours.

The Turks were now driving another mine against St Michael, and Matias de Rivera entered it, armed only with a dagger. Having thoroughly examined it, he came back and made his report. Meanwhile they were building another siege weapon, a tower made of wood, opposite St Michael in order to command our fortifications. But we blew it down with the same gun that had destroyed their *manta*. This day our parish priest, who was ill in bed, sent a message to the prior of the church, to tell the Grand Master that he should not fear for the loss of Birgu, for he would soon have good reason to rejoice.

Balbi dismisses the destruction of this siege tower in a brief word, but Cirni Corso and other historians of the siege show it to have been one of the most exciting incidents in the whole story. The tower was manned by Janissary sharpshooters who were picking off the defenders within the ruined walls. The cannon in its concealed opening was silently loaded with chain-shot, then, at a given moment, the stones that hid the gun muzzle were knocked away, and it opened fire at point-blank range. The tower supports began to buckle and, as the Janissaries threw themselves to the ground in an effort to escape, a raiding party dashed out and massacred them. The ruins of the siege tower were now occupied by the defenders, as a sniping post against the Turks.

Monday, 3 September. Forty galleys left Marsamuscetto and went up to Comino. They came back the same night laden with brushwood, which seemed to indicate that the Turks were going to build new trenches and gun platforms.

Tuesday, 4 September. At dawn, having failed in all their objectives, the enemy opened fire on St Michael. Since they had few guns left for bombardment they fired them off as rapidly as possible.

Wednesday, 5 September. The Turks kept up a furious bombardment both of St Michael and the Post of Castile. But despite this, we noticed every day they were embarking their stores and withdrawing their artillery. Naturally this put great heart into us. Yet all the same we were distressed because, if only the relief force of the Catholic

King arrived soon, we hoped to get our hands on their siege guns.

Thursday, 6 September. The Turks dragged two heavy guns into the Bormla area, and with them they began to bombard the Post of Martello, the houses, and the large merchant ship. Up to now they had never fired upon this ship, because they had hoped to capture it intact.

For our part, as soon as we saw that they were bombarding the ship, we felt confident that they were about to leave, and that they had news of our relief force being on the way. So that the merchantman should not sink, the Grand Master had a number of hawsers passed around her. These were made fast to the shore with a great many ships' anchors, and in this way we managed to save the vessel.

It was on this day, nevertheless, that the bread ration of both the soldiers and knights was reduced in some of the Auberges, which made us think that the Grand Master still anticipated a long siege. Another thing that happened was that we saw a Turk, who seemed to be an officer, loading a gun with his own hands on the Salvador gun platform. Clearly the gun was still hot for, when he put in the second charge, it exploded, killing him and the men round about. After this there was no more firing from that gun platform. Overnight our soldiers sallied out from Castile and St Michael into the Turkish trenches, but they found no one in them – only some cloaks and shovels which they brought back. This sortie clearly revealed how weak and demoralized the enemy were, since they were not prepared to stay in their trenches at night. They were also afraid to keep their galleys in the harbour, and in order to man them they were forced to withdraw men from their trenches.

The large merchantman mentioned here was the one which had been captured by Romegas, that great sailor of the Order, and whose loss had so infuriated the sultan's court. Throughout the siege it was moored alongside Birgu, as is shown in one of the paintings by Matteo Perez di Allecio to be seen in the National Museum, Valetta. These paintings were executed within the lifetime of survivors from the great siege, and on their instructions, so that they may be taken as accurate representations of events in the siege, and of the disposition of the various forces. A set of engravings from them in the Royal Malta Library is dated 1582.

Friday, 7 September. Throughout the siege Our Lord in His infinite mercy always helped and protected us, but especially so on this day, the eve of the Nativity of the Virgin Mary, the Mother of God. The Janissaries and Spahis who remained had entered their trenches, ready for a final assault, but Our Lord saw to it that, just as they were about to attack, a quarrel broke amongst them. They left their trenches and went to see the pashas, and we learned later that this all arose because not one of them was willing to be the first over the top.

While this was going on, our watchmen on St Angelo made out a galleot coming from the direction of Gozo. It went into Marsamuscetto at full speed, and at once a blank shot was fired from St Elmo. Shortly afterwards the watchers on the Posts of Germany, England, and Castile, saw a Turk disembark from a small boat at Rinella. A horse was led up to him but when he mounted, either out of clumsiness or nerves, he fell off. Getting up again, he drew his scimitar, cut off the horse's legs, and then went on foot, together with an escort, to the valley of Kalkara where Mustapha Pasha had his tent. No sooner had this Turk made his report than they all left their trenches, some making for Rinella (where boats were waiting to take them over to Marsamuscetto), others running over Corradino heights in the direction of their main fleet.

Shortly after this, thirty-five galleys left Marsamuscetto under sail, and formed up at the mouth of the harbour. We now realized that relief was at hand, and how overjoyed we were at the thought of regaining our safety and our liberty! By now the watchers on the walls of St Angelo, and on the bastions of Auvergne and Provence, had seen the fleet of our mighty and Catholic King, Philip II. Great was our joy when we saw their signal. To show how we felt, we jumped upon the ramparts, for there were no Turks either in the trenches or manning the batteries to fire at us; they were fully occupied withdrawing their tents and baggage to their ships and, such was their haste and panic, that if only we had had two thousand men at that moment we should certainly have captured their artillery. As soon as our fleet was in a position where we could see it clearly, each galley fired three rounds, but we, for our part, did not reply. We had no powder to waste and we could not yet be certain of the outcome.

After firing this salvo our ships set off under full sail in the direction of Sicily.* As soon as the Turks saw this and the direction in which our fleet was going, their galleys put back into the harbour and they began to disembark their troops again. In great haste and in

* Although Balbi did not know it at the time, the relief force had already been landed in the north of the island. The fleet was now on its way back to Sicily to embark more men.

confusion they started withdrawing their siege-guns and their tents. They worked so hard that, by the next day, there were only the two big guns left at Bormla, and all their gun platforms had been set on fire.

That night Grand Master La Valette had good reason to believe that, according to normal tactics, if the fleet had landed the relief force, they would surely attack the Turks during the dark hours. With this in mind, he reckoned that if we were to sally out from Birgu and St Michael, we would cause panic and confusion among the enemy and force them to leave their guns behind. Accordingly he sent the knight Gabriel Gort to St Michael in the greatest possible secrecy, to tell the marshal what he intended and to order him to have all the captains and their men ready.* Every man was to be provided with powder and shot, and slow-matches. The marshal begged the Grand Master to allow him to go out at the head of his troops and La Valette replied that if he definitely decided on the sortie, he would make him a signal. If our relief force, or any part of it, had indeed appeared that night, there is no doubt that it would have achieved complete success. Some of our men did go out from the Post of Castile into the Turkish trenches and, finding no one in them, they broke them up, along with those at the mouth of the ditch.

Saturday, 8 September. Never, I believe, did music sound so sweet to human ears as did the peal of our bells on this day, the Nativity of Our Lady. For the Grand Master ordered them to be rung at the hour when we normally stood to arms, and for the past three months we had only heard them ring as a signal of alarm. But now they rang for Pontifical High Mass, which was solemnly celebrated as we gave thanks to Our Lord God and His Holy Mother for the mercy vouchsafed to us.

During the day a renegade came over to us, with the information that the relief force had landed. He believed it was a very strong one, although the rumour had been spread in the Turkish camp that it only consisted of four thousand men. Seeing that there was no danger from the Turkish artillery, the Grand Master gave orders that we should bring out the three galleys that were in the ditch of St Angelo and get their armament aboard. Throughout the whole of the day not a single Turk was to be seen in their trenches, although there

* Gabriel Gort, of the Langue of Aragon, survived the siege, and it is a strange coincidence that during the next great siege of Malta in the Second World War, the island's Governor-General was the famous British soldier, General 'Tiger' Gort, V.C.

THE ARRIVAL OF THE RELIEF FORCE

were over two thousand in the houses of Bormla, keeping a watch over one of their large guns. This was one which had been taken off its carriage, but because it was so heavy they were neither able to get it back on its wheel, nor withdraw it as it stood; it was nine palms in circumference at the breech, fifteen palms long, and one palm in calibre.

During the night Commander Antonio Maldonado, together with the knights Juan Garces and Miguel de Marzilla, came down from Mdina to Birgu, entering by the Post of Castile. They told the Grand Master all about the relief force which had disembarked, adding that Don Garcia had led it in person to Malta. They told him the names of the important persons in the force, and how the landing had taken place. They went on to say that His Illustrious Highness, Don John of Austria, brother of the most powerful and Catholic King, young though he was, had been inspired secretly to leave the court and join this great expedition. But, they said, after Don John had waited many days at Barcelona for a passage, seeing that no galleys came, he had gone back to the court in deference to the orders of the king. This brave intention argues well for the spirit and valour of this prince, if Our Lord shall be pleased to preserve his life.*

Balbi now moves backwards in time to describe the embarkation and landing of the relief force.

On Friday, 24 August, Don Garcia had been in Syracuse with fifty-eight galleys and a large fleet of barges, which had been made ready on his orders for the swift disembarkation of troops. Together with him were all the gentlemen, knights, and adventurers who had come from every country to join the expedition. A council was then held to discuss plans for coming to the relief of Malta.

As a result it was agreed that Don Garcia should first send someone to the island of Gozo, so that he could make signals to the fleet as to which was the best place to land. Giovanni Andrea Doria volunteered to go himself and discover the situation in Malta. Delighted that so distinguished a man, and one so experienced, should be prepared to hazard himself, Don Garcia gave orders that

---

* This was the celebrated Don John of Austria who, six years later at the Battle of Lepanto, was to rout the Turkish fleet at the head of the combined Christian fleet. In this famous action the great sailor Romegas was in charge of the galleys of the Order of St John.

Martinez de Oliventia, who had been to Malta on other occasions during the siege, should accompany him. He was to take with him instructions for the Grand Master regarding the signals that would be necessary. These were, that if there were no Turkish ships to the westward one fire should be lit every night; if there were ten ships, two fires were to be lit; and for each group of over ten ships, an additional fire. To show in what quarter they were lying it was arranged that a man with a torch in his hand should run in that direction. Giovanni Andrea Doria then set sail in his well-armed flagship, his orders being to land Martinez in Gozo, and then go on to the island of Linosa where he was to wait for Don Garcia.

It was on Saturday, 25 August, that Don Garcia embarked six thousand Spanish soldiers; one thousand seven hundred of them from the Lombard regiment commanded by Don Sancho de Londoño, and two thousand eight hundred from the Neapolitan regiment commanded by Julian Romero; and the Sardinian regiment commanded by Don Gonzalo de Bracamonte. There were also some picked troops from Spain, but most of these stayed behind in Sicily with their three captains, together with the baggage and the young troops, as well as all the sick. At the same time, he embarked one thousand five hundred Italians out of the four thousand that Chiapino Nitelli had raised in Tuscany; they were commanded by his son-in-law, Vincenzo Vitelli.

Don Garcia had used all the influence of King Philip to prevail upon Pope Pius IV, to give permission for Ascanio Della Corña to join in the expedition. He was a brave and able soldier – as he had shown himself on many occasions – who at that time was held a prisoner in the castle of St Angelo in Rome. Don Garcia was finally successful in securing his release.

After he had embarked his troops and the knights, Don Garcia left Syracuse. All the galleys were without lights, and carried no boats on board, but each one towed one of the barges behind it. They had not gone more than two leagues when they were held up by a contrary wind, with the result that many adventurers, who had been left ashore, managed to catch up with the fleet and embark. Over eight thousand sacks of biscuit were among the stores, as well as a great amount of gunpowder, lead, rope, shovels, picks, and field guns.

When the bad weather was over, Don Garcia set course for Cape Passero, while Leyni, General of Savoy, went ahead on reconnaissance with two of his galleys. That same night Jorge Grimaldo and

Estevan de Mare arrived with their ships at Cape Passero, and joined the fleet, which coasted along the island so as not to be discovered.* On the following morning four galleys which were out on patrol were observed in action with a merchantman heading for Malta, and Don Garcia sent four further galleys to help them. When it saw them, the merchantman surrendered, and turned out to be from Ragusa. The pashas had sent it to Galves laden with grain to be made into biscuit. As well as this cargo of biscuit she was carrying a lot of rice and other provisions for the Turkish army. The ship, together with the eighty Turks captured in her, was sent to Syracuse by Don Garcia.

That night the fleet took on water in Sicily and then set course south-east in the direction of Linosa. By noon next day they were thirty miles nearer Malta. However, Don Garcia did not want to go there directly before he had had a report from Giovanni Andrea Doria. So he continued on his way towards Linosa but, with the continuing bad weather, he could neither make that island, nor Lampedusa. The fleet was driven before the wind as far as Pantellaria, where on 28 August, it was struck by a violent storm and they were in great danger of losing some of the vessels. The storm was accompanied by heavy rain, while the dark sky was lit by terrifying lightning and thunder, so much so that every one in the fleet cursed Don Garcia for, they said, they would rather fight with four Turks than be in their present peril. Many of the galleys lost their spurs [the projection from the fo'c'sle, to be found in all fighting galleys of the period], and many of them also lost their boats and oars.†

When the storm was over, by the Grace of God the fleet managed to reach the island of Favignana. Not a single galley was lost, and the Grand Master's *Patrona*, which was in the van on that occasion [though it normally came second in line to the *Capitana*, the flagship], captured a galleot that had taken shelter from the storm. Some Moors and Turks were also captured, and they said that they had fled Malta on account of the terrible hardships they had suffered there.

Don Garcia sailed over to Trapani to refit his galleys, many of

---

* By the Turkish vessels on patrol in the Malta–Sicily channel.

† The weather described during the fleet's passage from Sicily is very typical of early September in this part of the Mediterranean. Heavy thunderstorms and strong winds are quite common. In October, however, the weather often settles down again for a number of weeks until the advent of winter. Balbi has clearly forgotten that he previously said they did not carry any boats on board.

which badly needed it. There he took aboard water, left behind many of the sick, and set course again for Linosa. Reaching the island he found the two sailors whom Giovanni Andrea Doria had left there. They had a message for Don Garcia to the effect that Martinez was waiting in Gozo according to his instructions. Other information was that Doria had been in action against two small sailing ships – not so much because he had himself wanted to, but because Don Pedro de Pisa had insisted. He had come off badly in the action largely because Ensign Sarabia had failed to obey his orders. Doria himself had been wounded in the face by an arrow while standing on the spur of his galley, rallying his men.

Having received Doria's message, Don Garcia left some men behind in Linosa with a reply for him. The men were set ashore with enough bread and water for a fortnight, and Don Garcia promised them that if they should be captured by the Turks, he himself would ransom them. Having now made up his mind to leave Linosa and to land the relief force, he made his arrangements accordingly with the leaders of the expedition.

Don Alvaro de Sande, because of his courageous reputation, as well as the fact that he was a Spaniard,* was put in supreme command. Ascanio della Corña, whom the king trusted implicitly on account of his experience (and regarding whom he had given orders that nothing should be done without consulting him), was made Quarter-Master General. His Majesty had also given instructions that the Spanish colonels, the Italian colonel, and Don Diego de Guzman, who was leader of the Knights of St John, were to be considered part of the council. A majority decision was to rule, and all orders issued by the council were to be considered as coming from the king. Passwords were to be given by the Sergeants-Major. Don Garcia's orders [to the Commanders of the relief force] were given to them under seal, and they were to be implicitly obeyed until the Grand Master himself should meet them, at which point La Valette was to be obeyed as if he were the king. Chiappino Vitelli was to be included in the council because of his courage and his rank, although he had no special appointment. He promised Don Garcia that he would do all that he could in the service of the Order and of the king – as indeed he did.

The captain-general of the artillery was Pompeo Colonna, and Paolo Sforza was made general of the commissariat. All these orders were given in writing to the leaders who were told to observe them to the letter. A further command was that all the cocks in the galleys were to be killed, that the only orders aboard were to be given by whistle, and that the oarsmen should not place their feet on the chain-rests.

Livestock, not only cocks and hens, were carried aboard the galleys for provisions, and no doubt since they were going to relieve a besieged and starving island more than usual was taken. The reason for killing the cocks was merely that their crowing might be heard as the fleet approached the island, and give them away. Orders were to be given by whistle as being the quietest possible method, since in many galleys it was the custom to give the oarsmen their orders by drum, gong, or even trumpet. The instruction that the oarsmen were not to place their feet on the chain-rest was a further precaution against noise.

Having given his orders to Don Alvaro and Ascanio, Don Garcia left Linosa. The vanguard of the fleet consisted of twenty galleys, the

* It was natural to have a Spaniard in command since nearly all the troops were Spanish.

main body of nineteen galleys under Don Sancho de Leyva, and the rearguard of nineteen galleys under Don Juan de Cardona. This was their formation as they set course for Gozo with a north-west wind, and at the fourth hour of the night the vanguard drew near the island. By nightfall, however, the rearguard had lost sight of the rest of the fleet and, when Don Garcia was nearing Gozo, a short steep sea was running. Unable to see the signals that Martinez was making from the other side of the island (as he had been ordered to do), Don Garcia made up his mind to sail right round to a place where he could see them.* A little later, the rearguard reached its appointed position, but did not meet up with Don Garcia. Alarmed at not finding him, and thinking that he might have gone to Comino, Don Juan de Cardona sent a frigate in search of him. Don Alvaro came up and asked Don Juan what he ought to do, to which he received the reply that this was the place appointed for the landing, that he did not know what should be done, and that he had sent a frigate off to search for Don Garcia at Comino.

The frigate now returned without having found Don Garcia. This seemed impossible, so Don Juan de Cardona sent it out once again. Once more the frigate came back with the report that he was nowhere to be seen. Don Juan, greatly disturbed, decided to sail through the Comino channel and stand off from Malta in a search for Don Garcia. It was thus that on the following morning, 4 September, he discovered the main body of the fleet.† He brought his flagship up to the royal galley of Don Garcia, who told him to come aboard. It was only now that he learned what had happened. He was greatly distressed, for it was clear that they had lost a good chance of landing the troops during that night. Don Juan de Cardona stayed aboard the royal galley, while Don Garcia put out as far as he could to sea, so that the fleet should not be seen by the Turks. They were, however, discovered by the enemy that same evening, when they were in the vicinity of Cape Passero.

While this was going on, Giovanni Andrea Doria, having

* When Martinez had been sent to Gozo to spy out the land and co-ordinate the signalling arrangements, the assumption had been that the fleet would be sailing direct from Syracuse to Malta, i.e. arriving first of all off the east coast of Gozo. As we know, they had, in fact, gone to Linosa first – which meant that they were now off the western coast of Gozo and could not see the signals made by Martinez. It was this that led to all the confusion.

† Don Garcia had sailed round the north of Gozo with the main body of the fleet – rather than risk the somewhat difficult channel between Gozo and Malta, obstructed as it is with the islands of Comino and Cominotto.

waited at Licata, returned to Linosa where he found the two men left behind by Don Garcia, and the message that he was to go to Syracuse since Don Garcia was on his way to land the relief in Malta. Returning to Sicily, Doria found the fleet at Pozzallo and naturally thought that the relief force had already been landed in Malta – for there had been plenty of time in which Don Garcia could have done this. Don Garcia now learned from him that Martinez was in Gozo and that the coast was clear.* He heard further that St Michael and Birgu were still holding out valiantly, and that it was indeed possible to relieve the Order before all was lost. Doria told Don Garcia that the slightest delay might well be fatal, and that if he did not want to go ahead for fear of losing the fleet, he, Doria, should be allowed to go. He was quite prepared to hazard his own twelve galleys if he could relieve the island and the besieged. This determined suggestion by Doria made up Don Garcia's mind, and he ordered the fleet to take on water.†

What now occurred was something that is always likely to happen with ill-treated soldiers. A great number of the troops asked for their discharge on account of their persistent hardships – for they were dissatisfied with their food as much as with the sea. In view of the fact that the expedition had failed, they felt Don Garcia was not going to land them on Malta at all, but keep on transporting them about at sea – a life that appealed to none of them. In order to stop the men deserting, Ascanio della Corña and Don Sancho de Leyva stayed on shore to control them. But the discontent and lack of confidence among the troops was such that the coastguard cavalry had to be called in to stop them deserting.

On Thursday, the sixth of September, late in the day, the fleet set out for Malta. They set course for Gozo, hugging the coast of Sicily for reasons of security. Now as soon as he saw the fleet from Gozo, Martinez made his signals as arranged, and by midnight the ships were so close to the island that they could make them out quite clearly. Because there was a rough sea and it was a very dark night, Don Garcia sailed along the coast and then turned into the channel between Gozo and Comino where there is another small island [Cominotto]. Despite the fact that many of the leaders begged him to

---

* He knew this already.

† It is quite clear that (like Piali) Don Garcia was terrified of losing his ships. As the preceding sentences show, he had returned to Sicily after his first abortive attempt to land the relief force. It must always be remembered that in those days ships were comparatively rare and extremely valuable, while men were cheap and expendable.

land at once, Don Garcia was not prepared to risk it before day-break because of all the confusion that might arise.

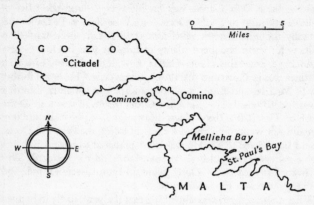

It was at dawn that the fleet came up to Mellieha, at the north-east end of Malta. Word was immediately sent to the Governor of Mdina, Don Mesquita, that the relief force had arrived. He was asked to provide men and beasts of burden to take the ammunition to the old city. Don Garcia also dispatched boats to make a reconnaissance in all the small bays, and to make arrangements for disembarking the troops and ammunition. They did this silently and efficiently, largely by using the barges, and within an hour and a half the whole force had been landed. During this period of disembarkation all the oars-men remained at their oars [in case any sudden Turkish attack should make it necessary for the relief force to withdraw in a hurry].

As soon as everything was ashore, Don Garcia ordered the galleys to take cover in the lee of Gozo [to the north of the island], leaving behind only the royal galley. He further ordered that the troops should keep close to the ammunition supplies until they had got them to Mdina. Before he left, he himself went ashore to see that everything was going according to plan. While he was ashore he suddenly saw the frigate in which Gil de Andrada had been sent out on reconnaissance making its way back.* Not being certain whose vessel it was, he re-embarked in great haste. But, as Gil de Andrada drew near, it became clear that everything was in order, so he said jokingly to the knights and captains who were standing near

* We have not heard of it before, but presumably it had been sent out as a scout to give warning if any of the Turkish fleet should be seen sailing towards Mellieha.

by: 'Now all that remains is for me to go, and you had better not detain me, if you want to comply with His Majesty's orders.' By this Don Garcia meant that he had orders from the king not to risk his life on any account. The knights and captains then replied that, since it was against His Majesty's wishes, they would not dream of detaining him.*

Don Garcia now re-embarked, taking aboard with him the brothers of the Marquis of Pescara. Having joined the main body of the fleet, he set course for Sicily where he was to embark the Italian troops belonging to the Duke of Urbino. They were already in Messina under the command of the two colonels, Pedro Antonio de Lunato and Giacomo Malatesta.

When Don Garcia was in a position where he could be seen from Birgu, he fired the salvoes mentioned earlier. It was this that let the enemy know that our relief had landed. One piece of good fortune was that, only two hours before the troops disembarked, Ochali had sailed out of St Paul's Bay with sixty ships, bringing his men round for the last major assault which they intended to make on the eve of the Nativity of Our Blessed Lady. If these ships had remained in St Paul's Bay, Don Garcia would either have had to fight or to withdraw.

After Don Garcia had left, the captains of the relief force had the ammunition carried up [to Mdina] as they had been ordered, and were the first to set the soldiers an example by carrying it themselves. There was not an officer, nor a soldier, nor a horse, that was not laden with some of the stores or ammunition, and they began the march inland in good heart towards the place where they were going to camp for the night. This was about four miles away from their landing place, and Ascanio Della Corña had gone on ahead to reconnoitre. But, because of the great heat and the burdens that they were carrying (in addition to his arms each man carried eighty pounds of biscuit), the weary soldiers soon began to throw away a lot of biscuit to lighten their load. As soon as he saw this Chiapino Vitelli, who was in charge of the rearguard, told Don Alvaro what was happening. A stop was put to this immediately, and Ascanio della Corña ensured that all the biscuit was picked up.

The relief force had marched three miles when Boisbreton and

* Balbi's report of the interchange between Don Garcia and the knights is the only real indication that he gives in the course of his memoirs as to the general feelings about the Viceroy of Sicily. This whole episode is clearly designed to show Don Garcia as a coward – as is the ironical reply of the knights and captains.

Vincenzo Anastasi met them. They were coming down with some horses from Mdina, and said that they were being followed by Maltese with beasts of burden to help transport the stores. They also provided horses for some of the gentlemen who wanted them. Worried about assembling his troops at the place he had selected for the camp, Ascanio della Corña urged them to hurry because, before they could reach it, there was a narrow path which is marked on the map of Malta.* Should the Turks land from the sea and occupy it, our men would be in great danger. Consequently Ascanio urged them on remorselessly, for he knew what might happen, and that only swift arrival at the camp could give them security. All the Maltese, men, women, and children, came down from Mdina with their beasts of burden and carried away the stores, so that by 10 September they were all in safe keeping.

This then was the way in which our relief force landed and finally reached Malta. I shall now return to my story where I left it.

* It is impossible to tell which map of Malta Balbi is referring to, but the path he means is almost certainly the route that leads up from Mellieha Bay through the high ground and then inland towards Mdina, which would have been an ideal place for an ambush.

XIV

THE TURKISH FORCES ARE ROUTED
AND THE ISLAND OF MALTA IS
AGAIN FREE

Sunday, 9 September. No Turks were to be seen in any trenches, except on the heights above St Elmo, because their fleet was lying in Marsamuscetto. By now they had already set fire to all their gun platforms and had managed to withdraw all their artillery without loss. The two thousand Turks who, as I have said, were guarding the large cannon in the houses of Bormla, had set fire to the houses on the previous night. This was a trick of theirs, for they thought that when the Grand Master saw the flames, he would think the houses had been abandoned, and would let the people sally out confidently from Birgu. Had this happened they would certainly have been no match for the Turks – who hoped to massacre them, or at any rate to gain some kind of victory. Their scheme failed, however, because the Grand Master would not allow anyone to go out, even though they begged him for permission. It was as if he knew exactly what the Turks had in mind.

The same day, seeing that their trick had not worked, a Turkish horseman came down from Rinella and ordered them to leave the houses. He led them to the gun platform on Santa Margarita, which they set on fire – but not before our guns from the bastions of Provence and Auvergne had caused some casualties among them. They were in such haste that they did not wait to collect their dead, but immediately made their way to the Marsa.

During the night we all rushed out from our posts into the trenches that had formerly been the enemy's. Not a Turk was to be seen. We placed guards upon them, as well as at the entrances to the ditches of St Michael and of Castile. At the same time we tried to bring in the cannon which was in Bormla but we could not move it because of its weight.

Monday, 10 September. As the road was safe, many soldiers and Maltese came down from Mdina to Birgu, since all the Turks were on the heights of St Elmo. They did not move from there, but posted guards and sentries so that, if need be, they would be warned in time to retreat to their fleet in Marsamuscetto. All the people who came down from Mdina declared that the relief force was magnificent, composed of outstanding men, soldiers of all nations, and gentlemen adventurers. They said that the flower of the Spanish army from the Provinces of Italy had been sent by King Philip. Their estimate of its strength was confused, some saying twelve thousand and others nine thousand men. This was something that we, the besieged, could not believe since, from the day that they landed, we had had no evidence of their prowess. Indeed, such were their orders, that I do not believe they would have shown any at all if the Turks had not forced them to it.*

I learned later from Ascanio della Corña that they did not immediately set upon the Turks for a number of reasons, the first being the necessity of safeguarding their provisions. If they had lost these then the relief force would have been in as bad a plight as we were in Birgu. The second reason was that Don Garcia's intention, above all, was to relieve the Grand Master and the Order by a show of force, and without in any way endangering the new troops. They were to make the enemy retire without an engagement. Another reason was that Mdina was nine miles from Birgu, and there was no water between there and the Marsa. They had every reason to think that the enemy would have dug themselves in at Marsa, and it seemed sensible in such terribly hot weather not to lead soldiers into a position where thirst alone could defeat them.

Although Ascanio's reasons were good enough, there was a great deal of argument on the subject, and it was said that the opportunity should never have been lost. It was well known that the Turks had been in Malta for four months, and that the island was so barren that there was no possibility of their finding provisions. Then there was the fact that the Turks must certainly have suffered heavy losses, quite apart from the many who had sickened and died [from disease]. What was more, it was common knowledge that, in the later stages, they had been forced to withdraw their troops from the trenches in order to man their galleys.

There were some who said that, immediately after disembarking, four thousand arquebusiers (having rested in Mdina and collected guides and horses) should have marched down to Birgu. If when they fired their salvoes our fleet with its light well-armed galleys had

* Balbi is quite correct in this estimate. Everything goes to show that it was Don Garcia's intention, on King Philip's orders, to cause a Turkish retreat without engaging in a pitched battle.

closed Birgu, the Turks would have been forced to send out as many of their galleys as they could from Marsamuscetto. This would have left fewer troops ashore. Our fleet need only have given an appearance of aggression, without in fact engaging the enemy. Had the Turkish fleet sought an action, ours would have had plenty of time to get away.

This stratagem would have kept the enemy fully engaged until the four thousand arquebusiers had reached the Marsa – which could not have been strongly defended. The arquebusiers together with the forces of the Grand Master – who would also have sallied out – might then have captured the Turkish artillery as the Grand Master had always hoped to do. Furthermore, we might have captured or burned the Turkish fleet in Marsamuscetto. The fact remains that, although men are always willing to discuss past events, they have no knowledge of what orders their leaders may have had from their princes, nor do they know their plans, for these are not common knowledge. In this way men may often misjudge their generals.*

By now the relief force had reached Mdina, and Ascanio della Corña billeted the infantry in a suburb of the city where there were two ancient churches, one dedicated to the Glorious St Paul, and the other to St Francis.† The gentlemen adventurers were billeted within the city itself, where they awaited the orders of the Grand Master. Meanwhile the men, women, and children rushed out from Birgu to the Turkish gun platforms. They brought back whatever wood they could find, so as to restore the houses which the enemy had either burned or destroyed.

During the night a Christian from Genoa escaped from the Turkish fleet and made his way to Birgu. When questioned by the Grand Master, he stated openly in the square that the fleet had left Marsamuscetto without leaving a single thing behind. They had burned everything that was not essential, including old ropes and sails, woollen sacks, and other material used for making defence works, so that we Christians should not be able to avail ourselves of them. But he went on to say that all their fighting men were still ashore, that they had provisions for three days, and that there were about ten thousand men in all. They had been left behind, he said,

---

* Balbi's arguments as to what *might* have been done are all reasonable. His last sentence, however, is a sensible qualification of them, and might well stand as a reminder for all later historians.

† On the east side of the old city, where the ground slopes down all the way to St Paul's Bay.

because they did not believe our relief force was more than four thousand men. Their intention was to lay two ambushes, one of them at St Michael, where they hoped that the news of our relief force having landed would have made us relax our vigilance.

He went on to say that these troops had been left on shore because of a quarrel between the two pashas. In a heated argument, each had accused the other of being responsible for the failure of the siege. Mustapha Pasha charged Piali with negligence, saying that if he had kept command of the sea as the sultan had ordered, the relief force could never have landed, and Malta would now have belonged to the sultan. He spoke no more than the truth. Piali in reply said that, as he had been given the charge of the royal fleet, so dear to the sultan's heart (and this had been impressed upon him), he could not take the same risks as one might with four miserable galleys. Mustapha, he maintained, was really to blame because he had had adequate forces to capture Malta, but had failed to do so. He, for his part, had been keeping a watch on the most likely places where the Christians might try to land.

After a bitter and protracted argument, Mustapha gave it as his opinion that, since they were sure a strong relief force had landed, the best thing was to leave immediately. But Piali said: 'What excuse will you give, O Mustapha, to the sultan? If you leave without even seeing the enemy, will he not cut off your head? If you have not seen them, you cannot even tell him from what forces you fled. This is why I tell you that you ought to stay with your troops on shore and try and bring this relief force to battle. If they are as few in number as it is said they are, you will easily defeat them, and there will still be time to capture Malta. But if this relief should be too powerful, then you can retire in good order to St Paul's Bay, where I shall wait with the fleet to embark you. In this way you will be able to make excuses to the sultan, since you will have seen the enemy and will be able to give an account of them.' Mustapha was finally convinced by Piali's argument, and took his advice.

No sooner did Grand Master La Valette learn what the enemy intended than he sent Monsieur de Boisbreton to Mdina to tell the leaders of the relief force what had happened. He gave them no specific orders, but just told them to act as seemed best under the circumstances. He also issued strict instructions, that under pain of death, no soldier who had been in Birgu or St Michael during the siege, should go outside the walls. Every man was to remain as much on guard as he had been during our moments of greatest peril.

Tuesday, 11 September. Now that he knew the enemy's intentions, and had sent Boisbreton to Mdina to warn the leaders of the relief force, Grand Master La Valette gave orders, two hours before dawn, for all the soldiers who had come down to Birgu from Mdina to report back. There were over a hundred of them, come partly to see the effects of the Turkish bombardment, and partly the Grand Master, as well as to get some wine – for none had been brought in the provisions that I have described. I myself went back with these men to see what might happen, for it seemed certain that there would be some action.

It was dawn when the sentries of the relief force saw the Turks advancing and burning down all the places through which they passed. The sentries reported to their captains, the alarm was sounded, and the banners were unfurled. However, when it seemed clear that the Turks had halted their advance, our troops were ordered back to their billets. It was soon after this that Boisbreton arrived bringing the Grand Master's letter to the Governor of Mdina. In the council that was immediately held, there were a number of different opinions, some in favour of seeking out the enemy, and others against it.

The Turks now re-started their advance on Mdina, laying waste the land as they came. The alarm was immediately given, the banners again unfurled, and the troops formed up into their

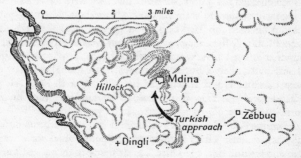

squadrons. We arquebusiers were stationed in a high, naturally well-protected position, and Ascanio della Corña thought that we should wait for the Turkish assault, for it seemed quite clear that they intended to attack us at this very point.* If they were to do so, they

* What Balbi means is that the arquebusiers were stationed in Mdina itself, which is on a high and rocky eminence, the land falling away almost sheer on three sides of the old city.

would easily be driven off, for we had every advantage, while they, in order to get at us, would be forced to climb the steep ground and would be tired out and dying of thirst.

But as it turned out, when the squadrons were formed up and the banners unfurled, there was such confusion and disorder that not even our officers could exercise any authority. So great was the general desire to come to grips with the Turks, that they could not restrain their troops even with their swords. Some Maltese now told Don Alvaro that if some arquebusiers were dispatched to a hillock behind Mdina (on which there was a small tower) they could cause great damage to the enemy, for the Turks would have to go past it if they wished to get to Mdina.* Paolo Sforza went to Don Alvaro and volunteered to take some arquebusiers on reconnaissance but, as I have said, so great was the disorder that Don Alvaro decided to send Captain Juan Osorio de Valoa and Don Marcos de Toledo to occupy the hillock, and to turn back the men who were rushing towards it in a confused mass.

When the Turks saw our men making their way towards the hillock they realized the advantage of capturing it first, and made a rush for it. But Chiappino Vitelli, who had also realized the same thing, got there before him. Calling out to the soldiers with him 'Saint Iago, and at them!' he ordered the banners to advance, and our men charged the Turks so fiercely that they were forced to retire, leaving us in command of the hillock. After a short breathing space, we again charged the Turks on lower ground and, although they were not far away from their squadron, they were completely routed. Known and loved as he was by all the veterans, Chiappino Vitelli was implicitly obeyed by all the troops, even though he had no specific command, and he acquitted himself very well. Don Alvaro de Sande and Ascanio della Corña congratulated him on his success.

Chiappino Vitelli now took a handful of Spanish arquebusiers and attacked some Turks holding a high point where there was a house and a windmill. He killed a great many of them, and forced all the others to retire. After leaving an adequate guard behind in the house, Chiappino and his men went after the enemy. Don Alvaro and Ascanio, seeing the disorganization among the Turks, ordered the banners to advance, while they themselves went ahead to take command. Both were engaged in the day's fighting, their

---

* This 'hillock' was presumably the ridge on which the suburb of Rabat now stands, a little to the west of Mdina itself.

swords well-dipped in blood, while Don Alvaro's horse was shot from under him by an arrow which hit it in the neck.

By now the sun was at its zenith, and the heat was so great that I maintain I never knew it so hot in all the siege as on that day.* Christians and Turks alike could hardly stand from exhaustion, heat, and thirst, and many died. When Mustapha Pasha saw that his vanguard was fleeing in disorder before a handful of men, he detailed a good number of arquebusiers from his squadron to cover the Turkish retreat. They were fresh and untired, and did their job well, forcing our exhausted men to retreat to a height near St Paul's Bay. Two or three of our men were killed by the enemy, and many more would have been but for the fact that on this high ground stood Captain Marcos de Toledo and an English knight, as well as others armed with swords and shields. Their presence deterred the enemy, and in the meantime Captain Salinas, Captain Don Alonzo de Vargas, and Captain Antonio de la Pena came up with a body of troops, who charged the enemy with such determination that there was nothing they could do but retreat.

Mustapha Pasha, seeing his forces in utter rout, jumped from his horse and killed it. Then, to put some heart into his men, he placed himself in front of his squadron and did all he could to make them keep their ranks. Meanwhile he gave orders for the fleet to close the shore (all their small boats and rowing boats were already standing by), to give him covering fire from their guns while he embarked his men. It was at this moment that our men, tired though they were, charged the enemy yet again. The result was that neither Mustapha nor any of the sanjak-beys, nor their agas, could check the rout. The Turks who could not get into the boats threw themselves into the sea. Tired and wounded as they were, many of them drowned before they could reach the galleys. The Turkish fleet now advanced their prows right on to the shore, while at the same time their artillery continued to give covering fire.

When Don Alvaro and Ascanio saw the Turks retreating in utter confusion, they realized that our main body might suffer casualties from the guns of the fleet, and called a halt. The Turks having embarked, our leaders now ordered us to retire. We had killed two thousand of the enemy, as well as destroying about four thousand barrels of water which they had ready on the shore. We

* The humidity in Malta is very high in September and, although the shade heat is not quite so high as in August, September is usually recognized as being the most unpleasant month of the year.

could not estimate exactly the number of their dead at that time, but two or three days afterwards the bodies of the drowned floated to the surface. There were so many of them that it seems likely they must have lost over three thousand men. So great was the stench in the bay, that no man could go near it.

Those of our men who did not arrive in time for this last battle, regretted it bitterly. Our losses were only four killed by the enemy and an equal number who died from the intense heat. Don Alvaro and Ascanio not only distinguished themselves as leaders in this victory, but personally fought with great courage. I myself saw Ascanio wielding a sword stained to the hilt with blood.

Chiappino Vitelli bore himself throughout as one would expect of so brave a knight. After we had returned to Mdina, our leaders were sitting on the edge of the defensive ditch round the city waiting for our troops to return, when Don Bernadino de Cardenas said to Chiappino in front of us all: 'How were things with you today?' Chiappino replied: 'There was little that I could do wherever you had been.' Captain Salinas then said: 'May it please God that I may always serve my king under such a man as you. I should never weary of it.' Chiappino made answer: 'Let us call it a day, Captain Salinas, for you have given ample proof of your valour.'

Less than two thousand men on our side were enough to secure this great victory. We took very few Turks as slaves, because, either through tiredness or cowardice, they would not get up from the ground where they lay, with the result that they were killed without mercy. The most important captive was an old captain of the Spahis who was taken by an Italian soldier, and afterwards sold to Ascanio della Corña. I must not forget to mention the action of one of the knights in the relief force, for it proves that in our day there is the same noble spirit as there was in Roman times. Don Bernardino de Cardenas was offered some water in a helmet by a soldier. Even though the day was so hot and everyone was dying of thirst, Don Bernadino, after thanking the man for his kindness, gave it to some soldiers whose need he thought was greater than his own, rather than drink it himself.*

After the Turks had embarked, their fleet stood off and they waited until nightfall. They then took aboard all the water that they

* This story must inevitably remind the English reader of Sir Philip Sidney who, at Zutphen in 1586, said to a soldier who offered him a cup of water: 'Thy need is greater than mine.'

could and, after sending away the Corsairs of the West,* they themselves set course for the Levant.

Since they began their siege of Malta, the enemy had lost thirty-five thousand men, including Dragut and many other notable men. They had fired one hundred and thirty thousand rounds from their cannons and basilisks. Indeed by the time that I left Malta, sixty-five thousand cannon balls – all of cast iron – had been collected in St Angelo. The Grand Master managed to collect so many so quickly because he gave orders that no one should be allowed to draw water from the cisterns of St Angelo unless they brought cannon balls with them. So naturally, as many people needed water, they picked up the cannon balls wherever they found them, and brought them to St Angelo. In this way more were brought in than if three thousand labourers had been employed.†

Wednesday, 12 September. The Turks had now left, and the leaders of the relief force went to Birgu, as much to see Grand Master La Valette as to see the enormous damage to our battlements. These were so ruined that even the oldest veterans were astounded. The Grand Master received all the knights who came to visit him with great affection, treating each one as befitted his rank. He thanked them all according to their merits for what they had done for the love of God and the Order of St John.

Friday, 14 September. At midday we sighted our fleet coming down from Sicily with the troops of the Duke of Urbino aboard. On the previous day while at sea, they had sighted the Turkish fleet. Although handicapped by the ships and barges which they were towing, Don Garcia turned back the galleys and went into the Port of Syracuse.‡ Here he disembarked the troops, and after cleaning the bottoms of the ships, he set out again for Malta.

Don Garcia arrived in Grand Harbour on 14 September, at the hour of Vespers, with all vessels dressed with their colourful ensigns. As the ships passed between St Elmo and St Angelo, they fired a salute, and the two fortresses and the bastions of Auvergne and

---

* The 'Corsairs of the West' were the pirates of the Barbary Coast and the troops who had been under the command of Dragut and the Ruler of Algiers.

† Cannon balls dating from the siege are still sometimes dredged up in Grand Harbour. A considerable number were recovered during dredging operations off St Elmo a few years ago.

‡ Don Garcia could easily have proceeded on his course to Malta with the barges towed behind his galleys. There was no danger of his being attacked by the demoralized Turkish fleet. He could even have slipped his barges and attacked the Turks. However, in accordance with his pusillanimous nature, he did neither.

Provence gladly replied. As soon as he saw our fleet nearing the harbour, the Grand Master came down from his palace, surrounded by the knights of the Order and by those who had come in the relief force, and he made his way to St Angelo where he waited to receive Don Garcia.

The moment the fleet reached the point where the general was to disembark, the ships fired another salute and as Don Garcia stepped into his boat the fortresses replied. The Grand Master, who was waiting at the landing stage, jumped into the boat to receive him, as soon as it came alongside. It was with great affection that these two gentlemen greeted each other, and all of those present were deeply moved. After embracing Don Garcia, the Grand Master embraced Prince Doria with as much affection as if he had been his own son, for he knew well how much the prince had done in the service of the Order. After warmly embracing Don Juan de Cardona and other leaders, he shook hands with all the knights who had come in the fleet, in order of rank. After he had received them all, he took Don Garcia and the knights to his palace where they sat down to a banquet, made possible by the Governor of Gozo, who had sent down plenty of fresh food, while Don Garcia and his captains had supplied the balance.

Now that the fleet had arrived, all of us who had been in the siege ate well, for there were supplies enough for all, even though they were costly. But we did not consider them so for, during the siege, a fowl had cost two ducats (and even at that price they were rare to come by), while an egg had cost one *real* and a half. As for other luxuries, I do not bother to mention them for they could not be obtained for any sum of money.

When the banquet was over, the Grand Master and Don Garcia spent most of the night in council. At midnight orders were given for the Neapolitan troops and eight companies from Sicily to embark immediately.

Saturday, 15 September. Don Garcia embarked in the morning but, because of the weather, he could not leave the harbour and was forced to stay until nightfall. It was said at the time, and confirmed later, that although they had three days' start on him, Don Garcia went in pursuit of the Turkish fleet as far as the Isles of the Monks, Stampalia, and Cerigo, in the Archipelago.

Monday, 17 September. Five of the Order's galleys sailed from Malta for Sicily, taking the troops from Lombardy. Among them were many of the most important knights, including Don Bernadino de

Cardenas and Ascanio della Corña. The only troops left in Malta were those from Florence, and less than half of them never saw their homes again for they died from the hard conditions and from disease.

Over two thousand five hundred soldiers of all nationalities died in the siege. Seven thousand Maltese, men, women, girls, and boys, were also killed, as well as five hundred slaves belonging to the Order.

During the whole of the siege only one man was executed, an Italian from Genoa. He was put to death for saying publicly that we had no chance at all, and that it would be better for us to accept the money and the free passage that the Turks were offering. No sooner did Marshal Robles come to hear of this, than he had him hanged within sight of the enemy.

This is the true account of everything that happened from day to day in the siege, as I myself saw it, and I have written it down with complete accuracy. I have not touched upon things which occurred in the council, nor have I concerned myself with controversial matters – for these are things which I leave to more inquisitive men who are freer to do so than I am. Yet, all the same, I know well that there is a great deal to be said on this score and that there are many sources of argument.

GLOSSARY

BASILISK. A large cannon which fired an iron, stone, or marble ball weighing from 50 to 200 pounds. So-called after the legendary monster whose breath and glance were fatal.

BASTION. A defence work which consisted of two faces and two flanks, all the angles of which were salient.

BREASTWORK. A defence or parapet a few feet high, designed for the protection of arquebusiers.

CARAVAN. A term used by the Order of St John to denote a year's sea-going duty on active service in the galleys of the Order.

CAVALIER. A defensive work, sometimes shaped like a V, usually within the main fortifications. Any defensive work that stood higher than the main ramparts.

CHAIN-SHOT. Two cannon balls or half-cannon balls, joined by a length of chain. On leaving the gun, chain-shot whirled round in a parabola. Used against massed troops, and in sea warfare against masts and rigging.

COUNTERSCARP. The slope of a ditch opposite the parapet.

COUNTERWALL. Any wall erected against the enemy. In siege terms, usually a wall erected inside the main defences as a secondary defensive system.

CULVERIN. A long cannon, firing a comparatively small ball but with a great range. Generally in the sixteenth century any large cannon.

CURTAIN-WALL. The part of a rampart, bordered by a parapet, that connects two bastions or main defensive towers.

DEMI-BASTION. A half bastion, with a single face and flank.

EMBRASURE. A gun-port, or any opening in a parapet widening from within, and designed for gun or arquebus fire.

ENCEINTE. The main enclosure or principal area of a fortification.

FASCINES. Bundles of sticks, rods, or brushwood, bound together and used in the construction of earthworks.

GABION. A cylinder of wickerwork filled with earth, used for fortifications. Also a large barrel used in a similar way.

GALLEAS. A large galley with three masts, and fifteen or more oars each side.

GALLEOT. A galley propelled both by oars and sails, but smaller than a galleas.

GALLEY. A vessel principally propelled by oars. In the sixteenth century almost invariably a warship.

OUTWORK. A defensive work constructed outside the main enceinte, either in or beyond the ditch of a fort.

PASHA. An Ottoman title signifying an Admiral, General, or Governor of a Province. It was divided into three grades of one, two or three horsetails – the latter being senior.

PORTCULLIS. A frame or grating made of wooden or iron bars. Sharp-pointed at the lower end, it slid vertically in grooves at the portal of a main exit of a fortified place.

RAMP. The gradual slope from the interior of a fortification to the level immediately inside the parapet.

RAVELIN. A defensive work detached from the main structure, with two faces meeting in a salient at the front and open at the rear. It was usually placed in front of a curtain-wall to protect it, as well as the shoulders of near-by bastions.

SALLY-PORT. Any small opening, usually masked or concealed, in a fortification, from which the defenders could sally out and catch the attackers by surprise.

SPUR. A wall crossing part of a rampart and connecting it to the interior work. The projecting apex of any salient.

TRAVERSE. An earthwork or parapet protecting a covered way. A double right-angle in a trench to prevent enfilading. A gun-port designed in connexion with another one to give protective cross-fire.

TRUMP. A type of flame-thrower handled by one man, and discharging a form of liquid fire. Sometimes combined with a musket so that small shot was also discharged. Similar but smaller was the 'fire-pike', which could be used as a pike when its combustibles had run out.